continued

For volumes in the NCRLL Collection (edited by JoBeth Allen and Donna E. Alvermann) and the Practitioners Bookshelf Series
(edited by Celia Genishi and Donna E. Alvermann), as well as other titles in this series, please visit www.tcpress.com.

PREPARING ENGLISH LEARNERS for COLLEGE and CAREER

Lessons from Successful High Schools

María Santos, Martha Castellón Palacios,
Tina Cheuk, Rebecca Greene, Diana Mercado-Garcia,
Lisa Zerkel, Kenji Hakuta, and Renae Skarin

Foreword by Michael Fullan

Principal Kirsten Larson and Marble Hill Community,
Thank you for your leadership and commitment to Multilingual Learners and for sharing your values and practices that have transformed lives,
María Santos

TEACHERS COLLEGE PRESS

TEACHERS COLLEGE | COLUMBIA UNIVERSITY

NEW YORK AND LONDON

Published by Teachers College Press, 1234 Amsterdam Avenue, New York, NY 10027

Cover design by Jeremy Fink. Cover photo by Marlon Lopez, MMG1 Design, via Shutterstock.

Library of Congress Cataloging-in-Publication Data

Names: Santos Guzmán, María de los Ángeles, 1952- author. | Castellón Palacios, Martha, author. | Cheuk, Tina, author.
Title: Preparing English learners for college and career : lessons from successful high schools / María Santos, Martha Castellón Palacios, Tina Cheuk, Rebecca Greene, Diana Mercado-Garcia, Lisa Zerkel, Kenji Hakuta, and Renae Skarin ; foreword by Michael Fullan.
Description: New York : Teachers College Press, [2018] | Series: Language and literacy series | Includes bibliographical references and index. |
Identifiers: LCCN 2018006718 (print) | LCCN 2018024501 (ebook) | ISBN 9780807777060 (ebook) | ISBN 9780807759257 (pbk. : alk. paper) | ISBN 9780807759264 (hardcover : alk. paper)
Subjects: LCSH: Immigrants—Education (Secondary—United States. | Children of immigrants—Education (Secondary)—United States. | Linguistic minorities—Education (Secondary)—United States. | English language—Study and teaching—Foreign speakers. | School management and organization—United States. | School environment—United States. | College preparation programs—United States. | Community and school—United States.
Classification: LCC LC3726 (ebook) | LCC LC3726 .S26 2018 (print) | DDC 371.826/912—dc23
LC record available at https://lccn.loc.gov/2018006718

ISBN 978-0-8077-5925-7 (paper)
ISBN 978-0-8077-5926-4 (hardcover)
ISBN 978-0-8077-7706-0 (ebook)

Printed on acid-free paper
Manufactured in the United States of America

25 24 23 22 21 20 19 18   8 7 6 5 4 3 2 1

Contents

Foreword

Preparing English Learners for College and Career is a brilliant book on a very complex and crucial topic. In Ontario, we have been successful in integrating English Learners into our public school system, so I know what it takes. English Language immigrants who arrive in Ontario—and there are large numbers continuously entering—pretty much "catch up" to existing populations in literacy (reading and writing) within 3–5 years at the elementary level; high school graduation is similar—steadily on the move upward since 2003.

So I was anxious to read Santos et al.'s study of six successful public secondary schools in New York City (five schools) and Boston (one school). I found a great deal of new insights because of the level of detail. When I think of complex change propositions—and certainly EL success at large secondary schools fits the bill—I apply three criteria: comprehensiveness (Are all key elements covered?); mutual exclusiveness (Is each main concept clearly distinct from another?); and succinctness (Is the resulting framework brief enough to grasp?). This book is exemplary on all three counts.

The seven design elements are powerful: Unified Language Development Framework; Ongoing and Intentional Assessment; Intensive Social-Emotional Support; Passionate, Strategic, and Mission Driven Leadership; Strategic Staffing and Teacher Development; Carefully Orchestrated Structures; and Strategic Family and Community Partnerships.

These design elements in action are supported, indeed fueled, by six values: an ambitious and focused mission to prepare all students; the mission guides all decisions; an embraced mindset of continuous improvement; shared responsibility by the entire community; high attunement to students' needs and capacities; and a strong sense of pride toward all cultures.

Each of the eight chapters further disaggregates the framework in insightful detail using examples and data from each of the six schools. For example, the first design element—Unified Language Development Framework—contains four components: alignment to the school mission; integration of content and language development; development of student autonomy; and orientation to student assets. The inclusion of student autonomy and assets is a critical strategic insight. Similarly, Chapter 2 on "Assessment" is succinct and comprehensive, including: a continuous improvement mindset; varied focus on assessment; and utilization of data. Passionate, strategic, and mission driven leadership contains these components: setting clear and achievable goals; demonstrating deep knowledge about literacy and language development; and supporting opportunities for teachers to learn and grow. For "strategic staffing," the authors drill down to: recruitment of teachers with strong knowledge and content development; classroom and school culture of mutual respect and learning; and openness to learn and grow as part of a learning community. And so it goes. Clear and specific, with the smallest number of key factors described in relation to the actions of the six schools.

It is no wonder that this strategic framework and these particular schools outperform their counterparts—77% graduation rate among EL students compared to 38%, 37%, and 34% at the borough, city, and state levels respectively. I cannot recommend this book highly enough. It is a model of clarity and essential brevity. It tackles the content and process of change equally and in an integrated manner. It addresses the big picture and small picture, but never falls back on generalities relative to the former, or gets lost in the weeds in relation to the latter. It gives us a roadmap and hope for secondary school reform in diverse urban communities.

A final word of advice: don't use the framework presented as a literal roadmap. The seven design elements and the six immersive values represent highly interactive and synergistic processes whereby the sum is greater than its parts. Nonetheless, this is a very accessible book on a vital topic. You can learn a great deal from it and you will be inspired to use the ideas. Get a feel for their use, develop your own versions, and then check back with the book's framework. Conduct a study session on the book and collectively draw a set of lessons that might apply to your situation. This is my kind of change book: clear and deep; causes one to think; and inspires the reader to what may be possible on a wide scale.

—Michael Fullan, professor emeritus,
Ontario Institute for Studies in Education,
University of Toronto, May 1, 2018

Preface

Six decades ago, in a flurry of policy and laws, this country saw and recognized the presence of English learners in schools. Congress passed the Civil Rights Act in 1964, whose Title VI declared that "No person in the United States shall, on the ground of race, color, or national origin, be excluded from participation in, be denied the benefits of, or be subjected to discrimination under any program or activity receiving Federal financial assistance." Congress then went on to pass the Bilingual Education Act in 1968, acknowledging the presence and the needs of English learners (ELs) and offering help to local schools. In 1974, the Supreme Court unanimously affirmed the rights of English learners access to a full and equitable learning opportunity in *Lau v. Nichols* (1974), requiring states and districts to take action. State laws began following suit, establishing mandates and programs to help English learners.

A lot has happened in education reform since, and we have developed a much deeper research base about language development, bilingualism, student learning, and systems improvement. The size and the complexity of the population of English learners have increased, and the meaning of "the opportunity to participate fully in society" (as contained in the federal definition) has changed with the ever-transforming economy. The Common Core standards movement has moved the discussion of what it means to be a productive citizen, and the demands on language have become better articulated, recognizing language as the principal vehicle for human understanding and communication.

Much of the attention on English learners has focused on the elementary grades. This makes sense because that is where most of the needs are evident, and in the higher grades, students who meet state and local exit criteria are removed from English learner status and blended into the mainstream. English learners found in high school are a highly diverse group. They include those who have been in the system since the start but who have not attained the exit criteria, many of whom are saddled with an accumulation of academic and social struggle, placing them at very high risk of failing high school graduation (the so-called "long-term English learner"). But they also include newcomer immigrant and migrant students. Some of these students (those who generally do well) come with a strong academic background in their home culture, but others come with histories of interrupted formal education and refugee trauma. Mix them into a high school, and you have a complex learning setting.

This book begins to shed light on how educators at the secondary school level can effectively address the needs of English learners by identifying, documenting, and interpreting the efforts of six schools that have been successful at it. As noted in the conclusion, these schools:

- value cultural and linguistic diversity and leverage students' cultural and linguistic capital for learning;
- deliberately hire and support staff with relevant backgrounds and experiences who are committed to ongoing development and growth and share the leadership's vision;
- develop strong and unified language development frameworks that integrate language learning, literacy skills, subject-matter content, and analytical thinking;
- benefit from the support of their districts and states, which creates the conditions that allow for tremendous innovation; and
- partner with the community and with local colleges and universities to offer students a diverse array of academic and career-advancing supports.

In these schools, what is remarkable to me, as someone who has worked on improving systems of support for English learners for many years, is the lack of leaders seeking a "silver bullet" solution—a curriculum or intervention program that can be purchased. Leaders think about the whole school and the whole student. Success is conditioned on establishing system and individual expectations, developing a depth of practice, focusing on student assets in language and learning, caring about the student, and engaging communities. These are elements that give dignity to the students by giving them respect for what they bring, and addressing the problematic cycle of remediation into which too many English learners are placed.

—Kenji Hakuta, Lee L. Jacks Professor, emeritus,
Stanford Graduate School of Education

Acknowledgments

This report reflects the hard work, collaboration, and dedication of countless individuals. First and foremost, we wish to thank the school districts, principals, teachers, families, students, and community members from the schools represented in this study. We express deep gratitude to these individuals who graciously spent hours answering our questions, opening their doors for our research team to document and capture the culture, practices, and learning that are taking place in and outside of their classrooms. We wish to extend our appreciation to our field study teams who spent countless hours traveling across the country, carefully documenting the tremendous work for ELs in these school communities. Our field study teams included Tina Cheuk, Rebecca Greene, Hsiaolin Hsieh, María Santos, Renae Skarin, Lydia Stack, Steven Weiss, and Lisa Zerkel. We want to extend our thanks to team members Magda Chia and Annie Kuo and members of our field study team for providing feedback during our revisions led by Tina Cheuk. Lastly, none of this work would have been possible without the leadership of Understanding Language's co-founders, Kenji Hakuta and María Santos, and former executive director Martha Castellón Palacios, as well as funding support from the Carnegie Corporation of New York.

Introduction

This book comes at a time when state and local leaders are seeking models of success with English learners (ELs) in schools such as those we have documented through our research, and as leaders develop state and local plans within the context of the Every Student Succeeds Act (ESSA) of 2015. U.S. schools are increasingly considering the educational needs of ELs like never before. New standards, most notably the mathematics and English language arts/literacy (ELA) Common Core State Standards (CCSS) and the Next Generation Science Standards (NGSS), highlight and elevate expectations across the content areas for students' language and literacy skills as well as their analytical practices. As a result, the standards raise the linguistic and academic demands for ELs.

In recent decades, and especially over the past 10 years, almost all states have experienced an increase in EL enrollment. During the 2013–14 academic year, ELs numbered 4.93 million and constituted 10.1% of all U.S. K–12 public school students (U.S. Department of Education, National Center for Education Statistics, 2016). Despite this demographic upswing and the new standards' linguistic focus bringing increased attention to the needs of ELs, these students still face a significant opportunity gap in relation to other students. For these reasons, it is imperative that schools focus on more than the development of English proficiency and address the root causes of the opportunity gap. Yet there is still limited research to guide practitioners in how schools can incorporate policies, practices, and systems that prove fruitful for ELs. The educational programming, policies, and practices illustrated by the set of schools in this book move beyond a basic notion of preparing ELs toward proficiency in English, to a dedicated conviction and drive that designs and delivers schooling experiences that prepare ELs to enter and succeed in college and career.

In this book we profile six public high schools that have demonstrated extraordinary academic outcomes for ELs. Through our research, we have learned that it is possible for schools and districts to build foundations that provide ELs with a wealth of options to realize their aspirations and potential. By illustrating the details of how school communities achieve these outstanding outcomes, the examples in this book aim to deepen the national conversation about how best to prepare ELs for college and careers. We chose to focus our study on high schools because so little is known about supportive programming and design for ELs at this grade span that leads to graduation, college readiness, success, and civic engagement.

We looked for design features replicable in public education agencies because 90% of the U.S. school-age population attends public schools (U.S. Department of Education, National Center for Education Statistics, 2017). Two core research questions drove our investigation:

1. What are some high school models that have demonstrated strong academic (and postsecondary) outcomes for ELs?
2. How do school communities address the diversity of ELs across their classrooms and create learning environments that fully prepare students for college and careers?

The six schools highlighted in this book were chosen based on their significant EL populations and stronger than average graduation and college-going outcomes for ELs when compared to other high schools within their districts and states. The schools are:

- Boston International High School and Newcomers Academy (Boston, MA)
- High School for Dual Language and Asian Studies (Manhattan, NY)
- It Takes A Village Academy (Brooklyn, NY)
- Manhattan Bridges High School (Manhattan, NY)
- Marble Hill School for International Studies (Bronx, NY)
- New World High School (Bronx, NY)

Teams of two to three researchers worked closely with each school to conduct site visits during which they closely examined the schools' values, design, and practices. These teams observed classrooms; interviewed and conducted focus groups with key stakeholders, including principals, teachers, students, and family members; and gained additional insights through interviews with school community members. (See Appendix A for a more detailed explanation of our methodology.)

For each school, we examined the set of comprehensive factors that affect how teaching and learning take place for diverse EL populations, including Recently Arrived English Learners (RAELs), also commonly referred to as newcomers; long-term English learners (LTEL); and students with interrupted formal education (SIFE). Our findings from this research highlighted common features across the schools that drive their success. These cross-cutting patterns can be summarized through seven innovative school design elements and six shared school values.

The shared values, as listed below, describe the beliefs that guide daily actions and decisionmaking, shaping how students and their families experience the schools:

1. The school puts forth an ambitious mission focused on preparing *all* students for college and career success.
2. The school's mission guides all decisions.
3. The school community holds a mindset of continuous improvement.
4. The entire school community shares responsibility for students' success.
5. The school community is highly attuned to students' needs and capacities.
6. There is a strong sense of pride in and respect toward all cultures.

These six schools redefine the possibilities and outcomes for their ELs in tangible ways through specific school designs and related instructional practices. Across these schools, the following set of design elements are embraced and adapted to fit their strengths, context, and student needs:

1. Unified **language development framework** integrating content, analytical practices, and language learning
2. Ongoing and intentional **assessment** with follow-through
3. Intensive **social-emotional support**
4. Passionate, strategic, and mission-driven **leadership**
5. Strategic **staffing** and **teacher development**
6. Carefully orchestrated **structures**
7. Strategic family and community **partnerships**

These design elements affect the schools' decisions related to their investment in resources. There is not a specific "formula" of success for any one of these schools. Rather, it is a school-specific implementation with all seven of these elements working together in a coherent way, undergirded by the set of shared values, that enables the ELs in these school communities to flourish and exceed expectations.

This book is organized around these seven innovative school design elements and the shared school values. In each of Chapters 1–7 we provide an overview of a design element, followed by evidence of how these schools have organized their policies, practices, and programming to support diverse ELs from a variety of language backgrounds. In Chapter 8 we conclude our book by demonstrating how the shared school values enacted across the schools in their local contexts create a supportive and thoughtful environment that enables ELs to excel. Appendix B is a description of the educational policy context of the school systems of the featured schools, and Appendix C provides background information on the individual schools. A glossary of commonly used terms and a list of education acronyms may also be found in the back of the book.

We recognize that across the country there are multiple terms used in describing English learners. These may include English Language Learners (ELLs), Dual Language Learners (DLLs), and Multilingual Learners (MLLs), among others. We have chosen English learners (ELs) to be used in this book, following the federal guidance related to this population (U.S. Department of Education, Office of English Language Acquisition, 2017).

With regard to quotes by individuals throughout the book, unless the quote is associated by name, we have chosen pseudonyms to protect the identity of the speaker following our research protocol. Please note that this study took place during the 2013–2014 school year, and some of the individuals who were present at these schools may no longer be there at the time of press.

Ultimately, this book provides a response to a frequently asked question from practitioners, policymakers, and researchers: How do schools succeed with ELs? Our research affirms what experts have long known—there are no quick fixes or silver bullets; rather, a variety of strategies depending on local circumstances and system capacity are necessary. Success requires systemic implementation and a dedication to continuous improvement. Success also requires a focus and intentionality on the comprehensive needs of the students—including their language and content development, social and emotional growth, and community connections.

The practices enacted in the schools in this book challenge traditional assumptions related to the assets and capacities of ELs. They also invite a reexamination of generalizations about best practices for ELs that have been informed by research not specific to secondary ELs. We invite you to gain insights into what makes high school work for ELs and consider how to bring some of these ideas to life in your school. Our aim is to shift attention to the possibilities in public schools to achieve success among EL high school students.

CHAPTER 1

Design Element 1

Unified Language Development Framework Integrating Content, Analytical Practices, and Language Learning

> The overriding drive in current changes occurring in second language teaching is the need to teach language through something essential and meaningful to the student. When the goal is to prepare students for academic success in classes taught in English, then English as Second Language [ESL] is best taught through lessons that teach meaningful mathematics, science, social studies, and language arts concepts simultaneously. (Ovando, Collier, & Combs, 2003, p. 310)

A key factor in the success of ELs in high school is the way in which educators at their schools conceptualize the learning of language, which we term a language development framework. One of the seven school design elements presented in the Introduction, a language development framework describes educators' best thinking—informed by research and practice—about how students develop fluency in a new language. More specifically, a language development framework lays out the implicit or explicit theories that educators have about what is meant by language and what must be learned and taught in order to foster language acquisition (Valdés, Kibler, & Walqui, 2014; Wong Fillmore & Snow, 2000).

For example, a language development framework may be informed by a definition of language as forms to be learned, such as grammatical rules, parts of speech, and lists of vocabulary. In contrast, a language development framework guided by functional theories of language would emphasize the use of language to carry out specific social acts and to communicate meaning (Valdés et al., 2014). Other linguistic traditions highlight the sociocultural and cognitive aspects of language acquisition. Crucially, these understandings about language deeply impact how teachers shape and deliver their instruction. In other words, theories of language acquisition and teaching have profound implications for the pedagogical choices that teachers make. Thus, a cohesive school-level language development framework—especially one that recognizes the language demands inherent in academic practices across all content areas—has the potential to impact how instruction is designed and enacted for ELs in profound ways throughout a school.

In our study of the schools in this book, we uncovered assumptions about language and language learning that permeated the schools. The language development frameworks that underlie the instructional practices at these schools play a large role in shaping the rigor of instruction, the use of the home language, and the integration of language, analytical practices, and content learning. Teachers in these schools integrate language development and content in every discipline to design instruction to meet rigorous standards. Teachers collaborate to align instructional and assessment practices, curriculum, and their professional learning so their students will meet the college and career-readiness content standards and English Language Development (ELD) standards. We saw teachers create goals for both content and language development in their courses and enact these merged goals in their instructional practice.

Within this design element of a unified language development framework, the essential components include:

- *Alignment to the School's Mission.* The school's language development framework is aligned to its mission, instructional foci, professional development priorities, course offerings, assessments, and other essential school features.
- *Integration of Content and Language Development.* Content-area teachers work with English as a Second Language (ESL) instructors to integrate content, analytical practices, and language development within their unit and lesson planning.
- *Development of Student Autonomy.* Teachers consistently use appropriate scaffolds across classrooms to support students' language development and strategies to foster autonomy.
- *Orientation to Student Assets.* Schools leverage the cultural and language assets of ELs to strengthen students' language and academic development simultaneously, through using resources from more than one language to make content meaningful and comprehensible for students.

How these components are actualized in practice is illustrated by the four schools highlighted in the following sections. We show the ways these schools envision, operationalize, and sustain a coherent language development framework for their ELs. Even though the individual school teams have varied approaches in growing ELs' language, literacy, and content learning, they all share the same attention to a cohesive language development framework that permeates the whole body of work in their schools. It is notable that they also share the goal of preparing students for college and careers, which is relevant to their school's language development framework, while some strive to graduate biliterate students as well.

BOSTON INTERNATIONAL HIGH SCHOOL AND NEWCOMERS ACADEMY

A major driver that shapes the teaching and learning at Boston International High School and Newcomers Academy (BINcA) is its focus on literacy across content areas and in all classrooms. (See Appendix C for further information about BINcA.) Every BINcA teacher is a teacher of literacy and content, and it is a community expectation that the core practices of reading and writing are embedded into all content areas.

Alignment to the School's Mission

At BINcA, the school week is organized with dedicated common planning time for teachers to work together in subject-specific teams, grade-level teams, and data-inquiry teams. During their weekly professional learning time together, teacher teams focus on reading and writing in the content areas as part of a schoolwide culture embracing literacy and learning. Figure 1.1 shows some examples of BINcA's shared literacy practices.

Figure 1.1. Sample of BINcA Shared Literacy Practices

WRITING

- We will teach our students to write Claim-Evidence-Analysis paragraphs and use them whenever appropriate in academic writing.
- We will teach our students argumentative writing as their literacy skills develop and use this whenever appropriate in academic writing.
- We will use at least two stages of the Writing Process (Prewrite, Write, Revise, Edit, Publish) whenever students write.

READING

- We will all use pre-, during-, and post-reading strategies.
- We will work to challenge students with varied text complexity and genre.

VOCABULARY

- Based on our students, the time of year, and the text and/or unit, we will purposefully teach words from multiple tiers.
- We will use personal dictionaries that include word, definition, and at least two additional columns as a format for teaching/learning words. Content areas will determine their common options for additional columns.

BINcA's set of shared literacy practices undergirds the larger theory of action and improvement that drives the work of the teachers. The expectation for all ELs is that they can acquire content knowledge, literacy, and language simultaneously in all classroom settings. The instructional team is guided by two goals that make up the core of their language development framework:

1. Cross-disciplinary and cross-grade literacy expectations for grades 9–12. The instructional team views this as a shared responsibility for students' literacy development. Courses include English as Second Language, English Language Arts (English, history/social studies), science, mathematics, and other technical subjects.
2. An integrated model of literacy in which reading, writing, listening, speaking, and language are taught together. These modes of expression mirror the process of communication.

Integration of Content and Language Development

During the 2013–14 academic year, the upper-grades humanities teachers recognized that they did not have a strong coherent language development framework that brought together vocabulary development, sentence development, and meaning-making for students. The team recognized that many of the language development sessions came together through classroom workshops or isolated lessons on sentence parts and vocabulary, and were not embedded intentionally in the subject-area coursework. As a result, the 11th- and 12th-grade humanities team, along with the ESL teachers, developed three specific language and literacy goals for their students: read, write, and comprehend complex sentences within subject-specific texts; utilize vocabulary development strategies to deepen understanding of words in context; and strengthen facilities with academic language both in meaning-making and use in academic settings. Within the 11th- and 12th-grade ELA courses, the teachers designed instructional tasks in which students work directly with grade-level complex texts, deconstruct meaning from sentences, and develop greater nuance in vocabulary, which they term "shades of meaning," as shown in the following example:

In a 12th-grade mini-lesson that connects sustainability in science and economic development in world history, students read from a *New York Times* article entitled "Where Do Old Cellphones Go to Die?" [Acaroglu, 2013] and spend time deconstructing the following sentence:

In far flung, mostly impoverished places in Ghana, India, and China, children pile e-waste into mountains and burn it so they can extract metals—copper wires, gold, and silver threads—which they sell to recycling merchants for only a few dollars.

Figure 1.2. Parts of a Sentence

Body Part	What Is It?
Main Parts	These parts contain the subject and the main action of the sentence. Answers "Who?" and "Did what?"
Lead-In Parts	These parts lead into other parts, especially main parts.
In-Between Parts	These parts fall in between other parts. They feel like a minor interruption in the sentence.
Add-On Parts	These parts give you more information about other parts of the sentence.

The class takes this complex sentence and begins to identify key component parts and ask questions as to how these parts contribute to the overall meaning (see Figure 1.2).

Rather than leading with a focus on grammatical parts of a sentence (i.e., identifying nouns, verbs, prepositions, adverbial phrases, etc.), the teacher guides students toward unpacking the meaning of these complex sentences so that they understand the meaning of each part *and* how they work together in contributing to an overall meaning at the sentence level.

In addition to the sentence-level work across each of the subject areas, the teacher-led inquiry team focuses on tier 2 vocabulary words that usually have various shades of meaning, are used in a variety of subjects, and are found in high frequency in academic texts (McKeown, Beck, Omanson, & Pople, 1985). The focal vocabulary "persecuted" was presented in the sentence,

> "They're getting *persecuted* [in Mexico] because as soon as they speak Spanish, people know they're American," Amani said.

The teacher follows up with the following set of questions:

- What if Amani said "mistreated" instead?
- Why does Amani choose the word "persecuted"?
- What additional meaning does this word carry that others do not?

Note that students are learning the various shades of meaning of the word "persecute" by examining how the word is used in various contexts. The intent of these language exercises is to develop greater facility in understanding how words come together to create more nuance and specificity in how authors communicate with their audiences.

The activities described above come together to help students build understanding and meaning from text, and provide them with opportunities to express their ideas and thoughts both in writing and in discussions. These examples of instruction brought together literacy and disciplinary knowledge-building with explicit language development. The new standards demand greater language and literacy competencies from all students, especially ELs (Council of Chief State School Officers, 2012; Kibler, Valdés, & Walqui, 2014).

This focus on working with core language and literacy skills has helped students develop into stronger readers and writers. Additionally, students have paid more attention to their word choice and had a better grasp of tier 2 vocabulary in their reading comprehension, writing, and discussions. Teachers also felt that the goals allowed for targeted conversations during their common planning time. Since teachers found the time that the instructional team needed in class to build meaning-making and depth of vocabulary was a challenge, the upper-grades humanities shifted to a double block of classes so that students would have more time to develop their English language proficiency and literacies. This allowed for use of more vocabulary-building strategies as well as students' continuous work toward literacy and language development in every aspect of the school day.

The decision for a double block of English in 11th and 12th grade is an example of many instances where the school structures, which reinforce the language development framework that administrators and staff have adopted, enabled teachers to learn from one another, problem-solve, and accelerate student literacies. Each department has two hours per week of common planning time that are built into the school day, during which teachers are not expected to cover administrative duties at lunch or in the hallways. Instead, they are able to devote this time to planning instruction, examining student work, or carrying out their data-inquiry work. Teachers shared that the focus on common planning time as a priority at BINcA has allowed them to deepen their practice and given more integrity to their work.

At the core of BINcA's language development framework are the teachers' relentless pursuit toward refining their teaching and learning through an inquiry and improvement lens. The teaching team develops instructional solutions that are aimed at accelerating students' knowledge and language development. These solutions are team efforts that are targeted toward the root challenges hindering student learning. The instructional team discusses what is working and what is not working for their students, collects evidence from its efforts, and revises and improves their practice based on student outcomes and feedback. This inquiry and improvement perspective is woven deeply into the fabric and community of adult learners at BINcA.

Development of Student Autonomy

In a typical classroom at BINcA, students are focused intently on their teachers and the activity at hand. Content and language objectives are clear and visible on the board, and the lesson's activities reflect an intentional design that allows students to express their knowledge through various forms of expression. Teachers prompt students frequently and deliberately, encouraging students to make sense of new ideas, wrestle with complex arguments, and help fellow students succeed. We saw a high level of student engagement due to the strategies teachers used to elicit students' use of language and leverage students' native languages, along with the frequent use of socially relevant topics as unit or lesson themes, such as the following:

In a 10th-grade English class, students move toward their table groups and begin working on the discussion pre-writing prompts about educator Geoffrey Canada's proposal to pay students to go to school in their writing notebooks.
On the board is the following set of prompts:

- Has Geoffrey Canada created an effective proposal to revitalize "The Harlem Children's Zone"?
- How do you know?
- What would you add or change to make this plan more effective?

Alongside the instructional prompts is the following set of sentence starters:

- I concur with the idea that . . .
- I take issue with the fact that . . .
- To make this program more effective, I would . . .

After about 10 minutes of individual brainstorming and writing, the students share in pairs and small groups their initial thoughts before transitioning to a large-group discussion led by the teacher on the merits of the controversial question posed by author Canada about whether students should be paid to attend school. For the large-group discussion portion of the lesson, students are provided with a handout that outlines numerous academic discourse practices and related sentence frames that can be used throughout the unit to enter into or continue the discussion (see Figure 1.3).
Throughout the teacher-facilitated discussion, students are attentive toward the speaker, and many appear eager to jump into the discussion. In this open-ended question of whether students should be paid to go to school, students are not in consensus as to what the "right" answer would be, but over the course of the hour, some students agree, others disagree, and some are on the fence and may be swayed in either direction. Using some of the sentence frames provided, students make sense of one another's ideas, practice making claims, and ask clarifying questions that extend the class's understanding on this controversial issue.

Figure 1.3. Student Handout for Academic Discourse

Skill	Sentence Frames	What I Said
1. Asked questions that propelled conversation	• What would happen if . . . ? • Is it justified for . . . ? • Do you agree that . . . ?	
2. Answered questions that propelled conversation using evidence and analysis	• In response to X's question, . . . • Going back to the question that X asked, . . .	
3. Connected the discussion to larger ideas (other books, other news stories, other classes or other situations)	• This is similar to/different from . . . • In comparison, . . .	
4. Successfully incorporated others into the discussion	• Earlier you were saying that . . . • Can you say more about . . . ? • What is your opinion on . . . ? • Do you agree with X about . . . ?	
5. Made classmate's comment clearer by adding new evidence or information	• To clarify what X said about . . . • Another way to explain what X said is . . .	
6. Verified the truth of a classmate's comment by adding new evidence or information	• I'd like to verify what X said about . . . • Her comment is accurate because . . .	
7. Challenged the truth of a classmate's comment by adding new evidence or information	• I'd like to challenge what X said about . . . • According to . . .	
8. Summarized points of agreement or disagreement in the group	• To summarize, X and Y disagreed about . . . because . . . • Ultimately, X and Y agree about . . . because . . .	
9. Justified own claim using evidence and analysis	• In my own view, . . . • According to . . . • This illustrates that . . .	
10. Explained why opinion or ideas changed based on new evidence or information	• After considering what X said about . . . I have reconsidered my opinion . . . • X's comment about . . . made me think that . . .	

During the discussion, the teacher takes notes using the same handout that the students have, and at the end of class, she shares with her students instances of their building on ideas or justifying their claims. Toward the end of the class, students reflect on which discussion skills are becoming easier for them, as well as which ones remain challenging, and the reasons they think this is the case.

The classroom vignette is just one of many examples of how teachers provide scaffolds that allow ELs to organize their thoughts, practice expressing their ideas in small-group settings, and then further develop rhetorical moves in advancing both their own and their classmates' thinking.

Orientation to Student Assets

One feature of the classroom experience that we saw frequently at BINcA is the consistent use of students' home languages—on the part of both students and teachers—to help students negotiate meaning and access the content being taught in classrooms. In one High Intensity Literacy Training (HILT) class for Students with Interrupted Formal Education in the Newcomers Academy, the teacher provides support for students in English, Spanish, and Arabic. In a 9th-grade physics class for newcomers, the teacher moved fluidly between English and Spanish in providing instructions to his students and prompting them with questions throughout the lesson. Teachers often group students together based on their home languages so that students can provide each other with peer support.

The students we spoke to remarked about how comfortable they feel learning English at BINcA because of their teachers' respect for their home languages and understanding of students' language needs as recent arrivals. The students reported having had at least one teacher at some point at BINcA who spoke their home language. Students recalled that they have never heard a teacher or classmate remark to them that their English level is too low. Rather, they embrace students of all language proficiencies and remind them that the best way to learn is by making mistakes and learning from them. As a result, students feel willing to take risks using English in the classroom. They know that they can always use their home language as a support when they need it.

The widespread use of students' home languages as an important tool for meaning-making and instructional support jumped out as a clear pattern within classrooms and in students' accounts of their classroom experiences. At the same time, students are accustomed to the norms of English academic discourse and oral participation as a common expectation in many classrooms. The result is a school in which students' voices and ideas are heard frequently and in multiple languages, and where students are not afraid to practice their English, knowing that their mistakes will help them grow.

HIGH SCHOOL FOR DUAL LANGUAGE AND ASIAN STUDIES

The language development framework at the High School for Dual Language and Asian Studies in Manhattan, New York City, is as the name suggests. The school, referred to as "Dual Language," focuses on helping students achieve biliteracy in Chinese and English by the time they graduate. (See Appendix C for further information.) There are students whose primary language is English and who may not have had any Chinese proficiency prior to coming to the school. Their interest in Chinese culture and language, and the school's focus on biliteracy, brings them to Dual Language. There are also students, typically with Chinese as a home language, who are former ELs and who have developed English proficiency over the course of their schooling. The school aims for a balance of 50% native Chinese speakers and 50% English Proficient (EP) speakers in its entering class.

Integration of Content and Language Development

A particular design feature that the school has found to be helpful is separate groupings of ELs and EP students in 9th and 10th grades and heterogeneous mixing of the two groups in the 11th and 12th grades. In the earlier grades, the goal is to help ELs accelerate their English language development, while letting the EP students focus on learning Chinese. The ESL classes in these early grades focus on language and literacy development in the subject areas, complementing students' humanities, history, and social studies coursework. Additionally, the school also organizes ESL courses in the sciences for ELs (e.g., Biology-ESL) that explicitly focus on both language and literacy development in core science subjects.

The grouping of students by language development levels in the 9th and 10th grades also allows for intensive support and guidance for ELs. In the beginning ESL classes in the 9th grade, the class size tends to hover around 10 to 15 students, and there is an average of 20 in ESL-content classes. The smaller class size, along with language development instruction that is couched in rich, authentic, and grade-appropriate content, may be a strong driver to the accelerated learning of the ELs as they transition to heterogeneous classrooms in the 11th and 12th grades.

Orientation to Student Assets

In the 11th and 12th grades, the ELs and EP students are in heterogeneous classrooms and have the opportunity to advance their language proficiencies together. Part of the school's language development framework is this belief that all students benefit from heterogeneous grouping that allows them to learn from one another—both in content and language. In both upper ESL and content-area classes, we saw deliberate grouping and pairing of students, allowing for shared sense-making of problem situations in mathematics, peer feedback in writing, and discussions of complex texts. For example, in one ESL course, the teacher created "high/medium" and "medium/beginning" English language proficiency pairings in an activity in which students gave each other feedback on an essay.

In an 11th-grade U.S. History class, heterogeneous small groups and the whole class could be seen doing a close reading and analysis of a Supreme Court case (*Korematsu v. United States*, 1944) and a Presidential Executive Order (9066, February 19, 1942), both related to how the U.S. government justified the Japanese American internment during the 1940s. ELs, former ELs, and EP students worked together to develop metacognitive strategies for understanding these complex historical texts, deepening their historical perspectives and knowledge as to how these arguments have been made in U.S. history.

This bifurcated model develops a strong community of peers who are learning a new language together—students who have shared risks, challenges, and successes together in safe classroom settings—and ample opportunities to engage in oral and written discourse in small class settings. The ELs gain a lot of efficacy, confidence, and agency in the 9th and 10th grades before moving into the integrated classrooms because they are all learning English together.

Development of Student Autonomy

Teachers and students alike at Dual Language agreed that oral language development is one of the biggest challenges of the student body. We saw numerous opportunities for students to practice their English-speaking skills through scaffolded interactive activities. During our visits to classrooms, we noticed that teaching practices were informed *by Enhancing Professional Practice: A framework for teaching* (Danielson, 2011), particularly student engagement, questioning, and creating a safe learning environment that allows for a range of academic discourse to take place. For example, in a chemistry class the teacher asked a mix of lower-order content and higher-order thinking questions, embedded as tasks, and as part of small-group and large-group discussions. Students were clearly engaged in processes where they were consistently asked to explain their own thinking as well as defend or refute claims made by other students. The chemistry teacher had clearly created a classroom environment that allowed students to take academic risks in classroom discussions, established safe boundaries of debate and argument in deepening students' understanding of complex ideas, and masterfully facilitated students' responses in deepening the class's thinking on the scientific concepts.

Across a range of content and ESL classrooms, we saw students engaged in various types of academic discourse, particularly structures, processes, and norms that reflected the tenets and ideals of academic discussions. We saw respectful and grounded discussion where students' claims, assertions, and arguments were guided by the clear standards of reasoning that are found within each content area. What was most notable across the classrooms observed was that each teacher created opportunities for students to generate ideas, challenge others, accept critique, and develop shared solutions in both Chinese and English in ways that allowed students to further understand the concept at hand. Figure 1.4 showcases some of the tools that students and teachers used in classrooms where we saw an abundance of student talk combined with clearly defined tasks. These tools and scaffolds

Figure 1.4. Sample Sentence Starters

Purpose	Sentence Starter
Clarifying something	• Oh, I see, this means . . . • Now I understand why . . . • I agree/disagree with . . . • At first, I thought . . . but now I think . . . • Could you reiterate (repeat) . . . ? • Could you provide some textual evidence?
Asking a question	• Why did . . . ? • Do you think that . . . ? • I'm confused why/how . . . • What would happen if . . . ? • What's your take on . . . ? • Why do you say . . . ?
Making a prediction	• I wonder if . . . • Since this happened . . . then I bet that the next thing that is going to happen is . . . • I think/predict . . . • Reading this part makes me think that . . .
Making a connection	• This reminds me of . . . • This character . . . is like . . . • This part is analogous to . . .
Making claims	• My perspective (or opinion) on this topic is that . . . • My conclusion is that . . . • Interestingly, I have a similar analysis . . . • Actually, I have a differing analysis . . . • From this, I infer that . . .

allow ELs, especially beginning ELs, to enter into the conversation and provide opportunities for students to practice, make mistakes, and reflect in the learning process. During our site visit, students "owned" much of the norms and sentence starters and were able to move fluidly in and out of discussions and debates throughout the school day.

IT TAKES A VILLAGE ACADEMY

The explicit language development framework undergirding the instructional practices across courses observed at It Takes A Village Academy (ITAVA) provides students with both challenging content and high levels of scaffolding to access that content. (See Appendix C for further information about ITAVA.) This framework reflects the Quality Teaching for English Learners (QTEL) principles where educators sustain academic rigor, hold high expectations, engage in quality interactions, sustain a language focus, and work with quality curriculum in teaching ELs (Walqui & van Lier, 2010).

Alignment to the School's Mission

These foundational language development principles are evident in ITAVA teachers' classroom practices and translate into positive impacts on student learning outcomes, as all teachers undergo QTEL training during their tenure at ITAVA. With these principles as a basis for their students' academic and language development, we saw teachers use developmentally and culturally appropriate teaching strategies to help students engage in meaningful tasks that reflect rigorous, discipline-specific content. At the same time, teachers can be seen supporting the development of discipline-specific language competencies that students need for college and career readiness. As a professional development partner described the integration of language and content learning:

> In most classrooms, if not all, you will see "word work" and attention to language going on in the classroom. Even if it is not in the lesson, it is there in the background and it is something teachers really think about when they plan units of study and when they co-plan about the language that students need to unpack the content.

ELs need extended opportunities to verbally articulate and build upon their ideas with peers. We observed students engaged in meaningful interactions with each other through intellectually rich content, texts, and tasks. Classrooms provided ample opportunities for collaboration among students with grouping and pairing strategies such as think-pair-share, turn-and-talk, jigsaw activities, and table groups.

Integration of Content and Language Development

ITAVA uses an integrated ESL and content-area program model wherein a content teacher and an ESL/bilingual teacher co-teach, and/or a teacher is dual-certified in ELD instruction and a content area. Whenever possible, the leadership hires teachers who are dual-certified. For example, a former physics teacher from Jamaica who is now certified in ELD teaches the Literacy in Science course. In co-taught classes, the ELD teacher may take the lead on lessons but have content support from the content-area teacher, and vice versa. This allows different instructional foci to emerge as teachers with different expertise take the lead, and helps each teacher learn strategies that support students' content and language development. The principal noted:

> The ESL teacher team-teaches with the social studies teacher because you have to push those subjects. They have to take those exams. So ESL teachers provide language support, content teachers provide content support, and they teach together. It also gives the opportunity for a social studies teacher to learn how to provide scaffolding, how to introduce vocabulary, how to differentiate texts we give to the students, how to differentiate questions . . . all those different components. You can provide PD [professional development] forever, but teachers have to see each other in action. This is where the real PD happens.

Driven by the Common Core and Next Generation Science Standards, language practices in the disciplines are coming into much greater focus. These new standards articulate the rigorous, linguistically heavy expectations that students should be able to negotiate complex texts, use evidence in text to justify their views, and be able to read, write, listen, and speak in the discourses of each discipline.

Development of Student Autonomy

In classes we observed, students were actively listening and building on one another's ideas, facilitated by scaffolding practices. For example, in a science class, the teacher read a complex text aloud with students, and then provided multiple opportunities for students to understand the meaning of the text in pairs, and then as a whole class. In an Advanced Placement Biology class, we saw students annotating an informational science text about an experiment that was conducted related to mussels and phosphate. The teacher asked students to interpret what they read with a table partner, share what the experiment was testing, and justify their answers with evidence from the text. Then students engaged in analytical class discussion about the text, and used their inference skills in the context of their own experiments:

The teacher asked students to share what they learned about experimental methods.

Student 1: The point of conducting an experiment . . .

Student 2: You need to have different control groups and experimental groups.

Teacher: Was the experiment set up properly?

Student 1: Not enough. There weren't enough variables in the experiment.

Student 2: I thought it was enough because they were just trying to measure whether phosphate affects mussels.

Student 1: Yes, it was enough. It was accurate because they were just trying to measure phosphate and they had enough.

Teacher: Why do we set the conditions the same except for the testable variable?

Student 1: When we set up an experiment, we have to set up the variable to test.

The teacher gave them one more minute to review the case study and then explained that they would go over the questions on the handout.

Teacher: What were they doing?

Student 1: They set it up and set the conditions for the experiment.

Student 2: It didn't tell us what the results were, but they told us what would happen if they didn't set it up right.

Teacher: Why did the students set it up with close to identical conditions, and what would be thrown off if they were different?

Student 2: Like the temperature of the water.

Teacher: Then you'd change another variable.

Student 2: It might change the results, and you wouldn't find the answer to your hypothesis.

Teacher: How would you change the hypothesis if mussels died in both aquariums?

Student 1: Well then, maybe there was something else affecting the mussels besides the phosphate.

Through careful questioning, the teacher created a student-led discussion to help them develop a deeper understanding of key scientific ideas (e.g., hypotheses, variables) as well as providing an opportunity to engage in the practices (e.g., explanation, questioning) scientists use to investigate the natural world. Students were conversant in the discipline-specific language (e.g., experimental methods, control group, experimental group, variable) needed to effectively engage in the analysis.

Across classrooms we observed, teachers focused on getting students to cite textual evidence to support their ideas. When asked about the standards, one teacher remarked about the importance of citing textual evidence:

> It's pretty much what we have to do on a daily basis, because we're constantly working with documents. We're constantly working with something where they're going to have to cite a source, they're going to have to explain a person's point of view, or have an argument for or against a certain idea. So if you're reading it, you're going to have to cite from it. Using primary source documents and knowing the difference between a primary and secondary source and knowing how to put all these things together.

As an example, using the graphic organizer seen in Figure 1.5, students were asked to answer questions about a text on Italian history, and to provide textual evidence to support their answers before sharing with their group. We saw a range of these types of organizers across the classes we visited.

Teachers noted that these graphic organizers helped students represent their ideas, organize their knowledge, and develop rhetorical structures. These graphic organizers served as the framework for students to practice rhetorical structures such as categorizing, inferring, summarizing, comparing and contrasting, and evaluating. For example, students in an ELA/ESL lesson on Lorraine Hansberry's *A Raisin in the Sun* were observed using graphic organizers in analyzing dialogue and character development from the text. In another classroom, students made their own graphic organizer

Figure 1.5. Textual Evidence Graphic Organizer

Answer the following question in complete sentences and be prepared to share.

Group Discussion Question:	
Can you elaborate on the reason why the economy was transformed in Italian towns after the 13th century?	
Your claim:	**Textual Evidence**
Your group's claim:	

highlighting the content-specific vocabulary and rhetorical structures from Chinua Achebe's book *Things Fall Apart.*

Eventually, students begin to build this valuable practice into their own skills repertoire, making them stronger and more competent learners, with the ability to make stronger connections and claims without the scaffolding. These graphic organizers support language development in that they encourage students to pay attention to the linkages between the content itself and the specific vocabulary and language structures needed to successfully understand the content.

Teachers also focus their time on vocabulary development and explicit vocabulary instruction in the content areas. In most classes, including mathematics, science, and ELA courses, teachers and students reference word walls with words that are essential to understanding concepts in that discipline, as well as academic vocabulary that crosses disciplines. Vocabulary is also developed in the context of texts while students are reading. This attention to vocabulary development in context was observed in classroom conversations. In a science class where students were reading about the Burmese python population explosion in Florida, the teacher read the text from the screen and then asked individual students to read the text and circle words they did not know. The students circled the words "non-native" and "disrupting." In the second sentence, they circled "food chain" and "reduced." The teacher then defined these terms in context, using the picture and other words in the sentence. In a global history class, students used a leveled reader to support vocabulary development and textual analysis, as seen in Figure 1.6.

MANHATTAN BRIDGES HIGH SCHOOL

The school vision of Manhattan Bridges High School includes the following three tenets (see also Appendix C):

1. Provide access to academically challenging college preparatory coursework in Humanities and Science, Technology, Engineering, and Math (STEM) to all of our underserved former and current Spanish-speaking English Language Learners to meet the demand of the 21st-century global economy.
2. Focus on developing students' skills in bilingual academic language and communication and career readiness.
3. Empower students to appreciate and use their native cultures and language as a personal and professional asset.

From this vision it follows that teachers at Manhattan Bridges share a language development framework that views Spanish as an asset that should be welcomed in the classroom as an instrument of meaning-making. To

Figure 1.6. Sample of a Leveled Reader in Global History

Annotation Column	Venice: Italian City State	Vocabulary
	Venice was **founded** in the 5th century by people fleeing from Attila the Hun. They settled on a group of islands on the northeastern edge of the Italian peninsula. Since the land was not very fertile, the early Venetians had to depend on the sea for a living. They fished in the Adriatic and produced salt from the seawater. They exchanged their products for wheat from towns on the mainland of Italy. They also traded **wheat,** wine, and slaves to the Byzantines for fabrics and spices.	**founded**— created **wheat**—a crop used to make bread and pasta
	Shipbuilding, however, was the primary industry in Venice. During the Crusades, Venetian ships provided transportation to the Holy Land. By the 13th century, Venice was the most **prosperous** city in Europe. The city became rich by collecting taxes on all merchandise brought into its harbor. Venice built huge warships that protected the valuable **cargo** of its merchant ships from pirate **raids.** With the vast wealth from trade, many of the leading families of Venice vied with one another to build the finest palaces or support the work of the greatest artists.	**prosperous**— rich and wealthy **cargo**— objects being transported **raids**—attacks on someone

Remember to annotate in the margins. Read carefully and underline words you do not know.

make sure they have the most appropriate instructional materials to serve their student population, teachers have worked in teams to create and refine their own curriculum over the years, resulting in instructional materials and teaching practices that are both engaging and rigorous.

Alignment to the School's Mission

Based on our observations and discussions with staff members, Manhattan Bridges High School purposefully and meticulously organizes its instruction according to a language development framework known as translanguaging. This framework celebrates maneuvering fluidly between multiple languages—much like a skilled opera singer shifts pitch—and values the varied fluencies of students (García & Sylvan, 2011). Below we explain the pedagogical theory behind this framework and provide numerous examples of how the school integrates this approach into its instruction and curriculum.

As described by one administrator, translanguaging is the practice of encouraging students' access to both their home language (among this school's ELs, typically Spanish) and English, so that they feel comfortable using either language to make sense of what they are learning or to express their thoughts. Because in translanguaging students formulate and strengthen their understandings using resources from both languages, they can attain greater mastery of academic material at the same time that they become more confident users of academic English (García & Sylvan, 2011), an outcome directly related to the school's vision for its students.

In order to strategically utilize translanguaging to support academic and linguistic development, researchers stress that this type of pedagogy must be "dynamically centered on the individual students' language practices" (García & Sylvan, 2011, p. 391). In other words, teachers should not treat students as a homogeneous linguistic group, but rather should be able to work with the multiple academic experiences, proficiencies, and backgrounds that students bring to the classroom.

To implement these practices, researchers suggest seven principles that support a dynamic, multilingual classroom environment (García & Sylvan, 2011). These are: heterogeneity, collaboration, learner-centeredness, language and content integration, learner-centered language use, experiential learning, and local autonomy and responsibility. Manhattan Bridges High School's ethos and practices wholly reflect these principles, and we explicitly illustrate four of them below.

- *Heterogeneity.* The staff approaches students as a heterogeneous group, and their instructional program is designed to leverage that diversity. Although Manhattan Bridges' students primarily come from Spanish-speaking backgrounds, they differ in numerous ways. For example, some students have been well-educated in their home countries, while others have had interrupted formal schooling. Some students are literate in their home language or English or both, while some are not. Some have been in the United States for part of their education, or have gone back and forth between their home countries and the United States. While most come from Latin American countries, the cultures within and among these countries differ. Family backgrounds are diverse, and some students are separated from families for various economic and political reasons. Thus, teachers and support staff at this school take great care to construct an individualized and dynamic educational plan for each student that changes as regular assessments show progress.
- *Collaboration.* Manhattan Bridges classrooms are highly collaborative places. In fact, the teachers interviewed related that they design

lessons so that students are evaluating and learning from one another. Heterogeneous groups of students were seen working on challenging, and many times experiential, projects in almost every classroom we observed, and all students were actively contributing.

- **Learner-Centeredness.** Our team saw students at Manhattan Bridges using translanguaging practices to actively and collaboratively construct content knowledge and develop analytical skills, with the teacher acting as facilitator. This contrasts with the traditional classroom in which the teacher has the main linguistic input and the students play a more passive role. For instance, in a Native Language Arts classroom in which students were studying the play *Don Quixote de la Mancha* (Cervantes & Grossman, 2003), the teacher facilitated a classroom discussion to elicit the characteristics of a play. Students then collaborated to create a rubric that would be used to evaluate plays that student groups would later write together and perform. The design of the project allowed students to become active contributors to meaning-making and knowledge-building throughout the project.

- **Language and Content Integration.** Evidence of language and content integration was prevalent throughout the school. Classrooms at Manhattan Bridges are language-rich environments in which scaffolds are put in place to provide students with opportunities to use language to access the content. In all classrooms, "content is the driver" (García & Sylvan, 2011, p. 396), with linguistic support being provided to access it. From collaborations between ESL and content-area teachers, to sentence frames, explicit vocabulary instruction, and process writing practices, students are supported each step of the way to master rigorous content.

Development of Student Autonomy

In addition to understanding the value of home language use in academic content and language and literacy development, educators in multilingual classrooms pay close attention to the translanguaging practices of students and adjust their own instructional practices to support students' intellectual and linguistic growth in both languages (García & Sylvan, 2011). This means helping students become cognizant of their own language practices in the varying contexts in which they engage so that they may become competent users of language in college and in society at large.

For example, in Ms. Y.'s social studies class, students were observed working with a bilingual text on the social structures of the Mayan civilization. Students were reading the text independently while the teacher moved from student to student quietly asking questions and then asking if students had any questions. Since the text was in both Spanish and English, the teacher showed the students how to use one text to help facilitate comprehension in the other. In one instance, a dual language student whose home language was English had difficulty with some of the Spanish text. Ms. Y. suggested that the student read the same section in English first, and then try the Spanish. She also suggested the student look for similar words in both languages, known as cognates. The teacher in this case recognized that the Spanish text was challenging for the student, and she used instructional strategies to help this student access it. These instructional strategies involved developing metalinguistic awareness about features that were similar in both languages, and about how reading the text in a student's dominant language and comparing it to the target language version can assist understanding it in the target language.

Orientation to Student Assets

At Manhattan Bridges, our team observed students' home language (typically Spanish at this school) being treated as an important asset to students' success in college and careers, as evidenced in part by instruction that values and represents culturally relevant subject matter. In accordance with the school vision valuing student language assets, the instructional expectations guidebook states that one of the goals of the dual language program is to "develop and draw upon culturally relevant texts, materials, and resources to facilitate and support the achievement of our Latino students."

Students themselves have internalized this inclusive view of language development. One student attested, "One of the goals of our school is to have English, and keep our Spanish too, because they know we're going to have more opportunities being bilingual. So they're trying to balance both." In keeping with this view, language learning is seen as a tool to facilitate understanding, not a goal to be achieved in isolation.

To help students build their native language skills, there is a focus on developing Spanish literacy throughout the curriculum, as well as through a strong Native Language Arts program that is aligned to the English Language Arts curriculum, so that students can transfer skills such as argumentative writing from Spanish to English. Students are expected to graduate as fully bilingual and biliterate users of academic registers in both languages.

One of the ways in which Manhattan Bridges encourages biliteracy is through the offering of AP Spanish Language and Literature courses. A teacher noted:

> [Students] take Spanish throughout [their academic career], because we believe this is a school to produce bilingual students. We want them to build up their English as a second language, but we do not want them to lose their Spanish. That is why we have a very strong AP Spanish program.

Like everything else at Manhattan Bridges, the approach to students' development in Spanish and English has been carefully and purposefully thought out. The use of Spanish as the dominant language of instruction in lower grades fortifies students' native language literacy and allows them to transfer valuable skills to English. Teachers use scaffolds in strategic and intentional ways to encourage their students to make the transitions from Spanish to English. History teacher Ms. H. walked us through how she integrates content and language in her classroom. She explained:

> There's an activity that we are doing today that starts mostly with images, because images can provide access in any language. We start the topic by doing a breakdown of things that they observe in an image—a conclusion they can draw from an image. Then we transition from there into documents. So we are putting English content language words into these ideas that they already have. In the meantime, they are writing about all of this and they write in English or Spanish. After they read the documents, they look at the images. Today they have to match images to documents and draw conclusions from both about the particular topic that we are discussing . . . Then they have to write a reflection, a comparison. Today's topic is the Great Depression. They are comparing the Great Depression to the Great Recession . . . [so we start] with something that provides an entry point for every student and then slowly build from there. They are working in groups, so . . . if it is something that they can't handle, somebody in their group can help them out. They always have dictionaries. They can always ask me to translate. . . . Those are some of the ways that I build the language. By starting at a point where everybody is comfortable and then building up.

Students are exposed to English in all classrooms, but by the 11th grade, they are expected to transition to primarily using English as they get ready for college. All the time, the norm of translanguaging allows students to harness the resources of either language to solidify their understanding of the material. Finally, the goal of biliteracy for all students validates students' achievements in both languages and gives them extremely marketable language competencies for their future careers.

CONCLUSION

This chapter addresses the importance of embracing a unified language development framework throughout each school. Although individual schools differ in their particular language development frameworks, within each institution there is a deep understanding among staff of the theory of action that supports their conception of language and language learning. Throughout the schools, four essential components of a language development framework emerged: (1) alignment to the school's mission and other essential school features; (2) integration of content, analytical practices, and language development; (3) orientation to student assets; and (4) the development of student autonomy. These four components are evident across all schools featured in this chapter.

The alignment of a language development framework to a school's mission is prominent in Manhattan Bridges, for example, as translanguaging is a practice that allows students to draw from assets in two languages in making sense of what they are learning or to express their thoughts. Given that the school's focus is on fostering bilingualism, it is wholly appropriate that students be encouraged to use language competence in one language to develop competence in another. The integration of content and language development is a component present in several schools, most notably at BINcA, where students are expected to acquire content knowledge, literacy, and language simultaneously in all classroom settings. Orientation to student assets is well exemplified by the High School for Dual Language and Asian Studies, where students, some of whom are primary language speakers of English and some of whom are primary language speakers of Chinese, are grouped heterogeneously in grades 11 and 12 so that students from each primary language background have the opportunity to learn from one another. Finally, the development of student autonomy is a prevalent component within ITAVA in the school's use of graphic organizers to assist students in independently citing evidence to support their ideas and in the school's emphasis on developing students' academic vocabulary for use across various disciplines.

The next chapter focuses on another key design element across all schools—ongoing and intentional assessment with follow-through.

CHAPTER 2

Design Element 2

Ongoing and Intentional Assessment with Follow-Through

Powerful instruction meets students where they are and gives them the opportunities to move forward. (Black & Wiliam, 1998)

Thoughtful and detailed assessment strategies form the second design element we found in high schools successfully graduating ELs college- and career-ready. These assessment practices allow teachers to adapt instructional materials to meet the strengths and needs of students, while leveraging formative assessment practices for continuous improvement. The practices also reveal a deep understanding of both language and content-area learning and include holistic methods that involve students in their own development (Heritage, 2007).

From the moment of ELs' entry through graduation and beyond, the schools we studied gather detailed data on students to inform decisions around instruction, course offerings, and school structures. These data come from a variety of sources: summative assessments from previous years, diagnostic assessments administered periodically throughout the year, samples of student work, and information shared at grade-level meetings or gathered through the course of interventions. Together, these data provide staff with essential evidence and feedback to guide ongoing reflection and continuous improvement.

In addition to collecting academic data, a guidance team works closely with students and their families, both formally through initial diagnostics and home visits, and informally through conversations and meetings throughout the year, to amass relevant information about the background, needs, and strengths of individual students and their families.

These schools value assessment not just *of* learning, but *for* learning, with clear achievement targets and conditions that support student growth (Stiggins, 2005). Within classrooms, teachers continuously use diagnostic and formative assessment practices to monitor student learning and inform instruction, yielding substantial learning gains (Black & Wiliam, 1998). According to Heritage (2007), formative assessment practices are powerful tools that provide information about student learning in relationship to learning goals and are important components of a comprehensive assessment system. These practices help teachers gauge where students are so they can adapt instruction to meet individual and rapidly evolving student needs. Teachers elicit evidence of student understanding and language use through a variety of techniques. For example, at the beginning of each class period, many teachers use a 5–10 minute "Do Now" exercise to revisit the previous day's learning and to reteach concepts that proved difficult for students. The use of "exit slips," an activity or problem assigned at the end of class to assess understanding of the day's lesson, was also commonly seen in classrooms, as well as quick writes to follow-up questions.

An important component of assessment is giving students the opportunity to articulate evidence of learning through a process of questioning and discussion that helps them to externalize their thinking (Darling-Hammond, 1997). Questions and rich discussions between a teacher and students or among students allow students to explain or expand upon their reasoning or evidence and how they arrived at a solution or opinion.

The evidence from these formative assessment opportunities is used to plan instructional interventions to better meet students' needs and to help students monitor and assess their own progress. These schools make use of holistic forms of assessment that allow students to take ownership of their growth and progress. Students revise their own work, present their learning via portfolio presentations in public forums, and work collaboratively on project-based learning tasks—all in the effort to learn from the process and from the feedback of peers and adults.

Within the design element of intentional and ongoing assessment with follow-through, the essential components include:

- **Continuous Improvement Mindset.** Ongoing assessment practices feed into a larger framework and mindset of continuous improvement in the quality of learning experiences for all students.
- **Varied Forms of Assessment.** School communities carry out a range of assessment practices in English that elicit knowledge about student growth, learning, and competencies that can be used to inform teaching and learning decisions.
- **Utilization of Assessment Data.** The results of assessments are fed into a feedback loop to impact the broader school approaches. Summative assessments such as end-of-term tests and state assessments serve as major benchmarks that are aligned to school goals and mission.

This chapter focuses on how teachers and school teams are approaching assessment practices at the student, classroom, and school levels in four of the schools we studied. The approaches at these schools vary, but all serve to inform instruction and advance achievement for ELs. In these school examples, we show how teachers and students interact with tasks and question prompts as well as tools that teachers use to support reflective feedback.

HIGH SCHOOL FOR DUAL LANGUAGE AND ASIAN STUDIES

Teachers at Dual Language embed Common Core literacy standards for writing, reading, and speaking within unit and lesson tasks. For example, science teachers prompt students to write explanations of biochemical processes, predict and justify outcomes, and explain pH levels, all of which are aligned with the discourse practices found in both the Next Generation Science Standards and Common Core State Standards. Teachers design tasks to include multiple entry points at which students could demonstrate their thinking about the content, allowing students to make sense of cognitively demanding and complex ideas through multiple approaches, both independently and in group settings. Unified language and content learning and well-thought-through formative assessment practices are major cornerstones of Dual Language's learning design.

Continuous Improvement Mindset

At Dual Language, language instruction and assessments were embedded within content-rich texts and course materials. We saw students grapple with grade-appropriate content that drew from their interests and/or connected ideas across various courses' content. Instructional planning is aligned with the larger school vision of supporting English and Chinese literacies in the school community, and the teachers design lessons with five interconnected components that come together to create a clear, guided learning opportunity for all students. Much of the lesson design work is influenced by Danielson's (2011) *Enhancing Professional Practice: A Framework for Teaching* as well as other resources (i.e., New York State Learning Standards) that have been adapted to meet their classroom needs (see Figure 2.1).

Mr. M., a biology teacher, shared his thinking behind planning for his ESL students:

> One of the classes I have is ESL 1 [low-EP] and the other is ESL 5 [high-EP]. There is a lot of scaffolding, especially with ESL 1 kids. I'll come up with different sentence starters and worksheets and help with vocabulary. Or I give them a chance to talk in Chinese. I don't speak Chinese. For ESL 1, I try to put a lot of visuals and pictures rather than just saying the word. I try to find other ways to express the words and ideas, provide scaffolds and pictures. For the ESL kids in my AP

Figure 2.1. Components of Strong Lesson Design

1. **Core academic content.** All classes, including ESL courses, are clearly aligned to the relevant content and language/literacy standards (i.e., Regents and New York State Standards, and/or AP course requirements).
2. **Cognitive demand.** Students are interacting with grade-appropriate and intellectually challenging ideas and tasks that stimulate productive learning opportunities for all students.
3. **Access to language and content.** Classroom activity structures create multiple ways for all students to enter into and engage with the text and tasks, develop deep understanding of the content, and practice with English language and literacies.
4. **Student agency and identity.** Through productive and supportive learning experiences, students develop stronger capacity and willingness to guide their own learning and learn from one another.
5. **Formative assessment.** The teacher designs opportunities to gain insight into student thinking and adapt instruction to "meet students where they are."

Sources: Danielson, 2011; Schoenfeld, 2014; Understanding Language, 2013

biology, they struggle with the textbook. I'm struggling because it's the first year that I've had ESL kids in AP biology. With them, I'm doing summaries and close readings of the text. I'm still experimenting with what works.

As Mr. M. noted, one of the major challenges of science is what some call "lexical density" of science texts. That is, science texts often are constructed with technical vocabulary, nominalizations, lengthy noun phrases, and abstract metaphors that differ from everyday speech. This "language of school science" is a challenge for *all* students taking science, and for ESL students, additional considerations need to be taken in how to organize instruction so that students can engage with the rich science content (Fang, 2006).

Varied Forms of Assessment

A glimpse into Mr. M.'s classroom shows the various ways he guides students to deepen their understanding of the biotic and abiotic relationships found in an ecosystem. Students have multiple opportunities to engage with and make sense of the content both in their home language of Chinese and in English, through writing and discussions with peers.

As the 20 or so students in Mr. M.'s Biology-ESL 5 enter the classroom, they see the "Do Now" that is posted on the board:

Who is benefiting or getting hurt in the following situations? Describe the relationship.

A. Friends help you out with homework.
B. You pay money to the cashier when you want to buy some snacks.
C. You forgot and left your phone in the gym. The phone is not there anymore.

Mr. M. asks them to jot down initial responses and then proceed to discuss their thinking in small table groups. Many of the students are speaking in Cantonese, although there are murmurs in English of biological terms such as "mutualism," "predators," and "prey," interspersed within their predominately Cantonese-based discussions.

After ten minutes of discussion, Mr. M. reconvenes the whole class so the students can share their thinking on these scenarios and how these human relationships extend into the ecological concepts they have been learning in class so far.

Because Mr. M. does not speak Chinese, the full-class discussion is in English. There is a sense that students are most comfortable in their native language of Chinese as they converse in small groups using predominately Chinese. However, in both classwork and in larger class discussions, students are encouraged to use English for explaining, listening, and responding to one another.

As the class continues, Mr. M. uses a multimedia presentation to highlight the various types of relationships that may exist in the wild. On the video screen, we see a female cuckoo bird swoop into a warbler's nest, kick out a warbler egg, and lay her own egg in its place. Just in time, before the warbler returns, the cuckoo bird leaves, and the warbler raises both her warbler eggs as well as the cuckoo egg as her own.

Mr. M. pauses the video and asks students to note individually the specific type of symbiotic relationship that is highlighted by the video excerpt. Students then share their thinking and are asked to discuss the relationship between the warbler and the cuckoo bird, first among their table groups and then later in a full-class discussion. Mr. M. provides the following questions to guide the students' responses:

- How do biotic organisms interact with each other?
- Describe biotic interactions.
- Explain examples of biotic interactions.
- Who is benefiting from this scenario in the video?
- Who is getting hurt? Explain your answer.
- Make a prediction and share with your group what you think and why.
- Explain how this interaction benefits the cuckoo bird.
- Why is this an example of parasitism?

Toward the end of the class, Mr. M. asks each student to complete an exit slip with the following prompts:

- Write three important things you learned from today's lesson.
- Write two things you thought were interesting.

The vignette with Mr. M. shows some of the guiding questions and tasks that allow the teacher to inquire and formatively assess his students' thinking throughout the lesson. Across classrooms at Dual Language, teachers used this type of ongoing, intentional assessment to probe at what and how students were thinking and adjust their instructional moves accordingly. Explicit in Mr. M.'s lesson plan are specific question prompts that probe student thinking and their development of the content while supporting students' facilities with language and literacy practices in his biology class. As a result, students had multiple opportunities to self-assess and reflect on their progress in and outside of class.

IT TAKES A VILLAGE ACADEMY

Teachers at ITAVA reported using formative assessment practices to plan instructional interventions, to change instructional practices to better meet students' needs, and to help students to monitor and assess their own progress. Many of the teachers use rubrics so that students can both assess their own learning and make focused changes to meet the expected criteria. Teachers and students use a range of tools to provide clear and direct feedback for themselves so that they can improve on their learning. ITAVA is an example of a school with a continuous improvement mindset.

One of the most important roles in assessment is the provision of timely and informative feedback to students during instruction and learning (National Research Council, 2001). So that students are pushed to ever higher levels of rigor as soon as it becomes possible to do so, decisions at ITAVA about what each student needs are continuous, data-driven, and based on individual student progress and needs, as opposed to static labels. Students may be moved from one class to another at any point in the year depending on their performance. Individual student progress according to formative assessments, achievement data, and other measures is watched closely throughout the year and discussed in teacher teams and among administration.

Formative assessment practices were observed throughout the classes at ITAVA. For example, the practice of questioning and discussion is illustrated in the following vignette of an ELA/ESL class co-taught by Ms. R., an ELD teacher, and Mr. L., an ELA teacher. Here, they are reading Chinua Achebe's *Things Fall Apart,* a story of Okonkwo, a respectful and influential leader within the Igbo community of Umuofia in eastern Nigeria, set in the late 19th century as European powers scramble for African territories, chosen as a text that is academically rigorous and relevant to the school's majority African and African-American students.

Students are sitting in table groups of four in this brightly lit classroom. There are multiple student-made graphic organizer posters hung throughout the room. In this ELA/ESL class, Mr. L. is reading aloud an excerpt of Chapter 7 from Achebe's book, *Things Fall Apart*. In the chapter, the village joyfully greets the coming of the locusts, a delicacy in Umuofia. In the midst of the feast, the main character, Okonkwo, is told by a village elder that the Umuofia Oracle commands him to kill his adoptive son, a young boy named Ikemefuna from the Mbaino tribe, as retribution for a crime the Mbaino people committed against those of Umuofia. Okonkwo obeys by executing the order, much to the dismay of his biological son, Nwoye, who has grown close to and been highly influenced by Ikemefuna.

As Mr. L. reads, he periodically stops to ask clarifying or comprehension questions (e.g., "What is a locust? What does it mean when the author says the bow snapped? What do you call it when you use a word or phrase to describe something else that's unrelated?"). This practice not only provides clarifications, but through metacognitive modeling also demonstrates how to actively read texts.

After Mr. L. finishes reading the chapter excerpt, both teachers direct students to begin group work. Mr. L. projects instructions on the smartboard, and Ms. R. verbally explains the instructions for their task. Ms. R. says, "Open your books to Springboard 3.11, 'Understanding a pivotal chapter,' page 162." They then model the activity and direct each group to take a question and provide an appropriate answer with supporting evidence from the text with a page number. Each set of desks has home language and/or English language dictionaries for students to use during their activity. The questions, which ask readers to employ critical reading skills such as drawing inferences, analyzing information, and comparing texts to other texts, are as follows:

1. How has Nwoye changed, and what has caused the changes?
2. Describe the arrival of the locusts. What is the reaction of the people of Umuofia?
3. Do you think that Ikemefuna suspects that he is going to be killed? Why or why not?
4. How does Okonkwo feel about Ikemefuna's death? How does Nwoye feel?
5. Genesis 22:1–19 of the Bible presents the story of Abraham and Isaac. What similarities and differences are there in the sacrifices of Isaac and Ikemefuna? How does this incident illustrate the novel's father/son motif?

6. How do you think the death of Ikemefuna will affect the relationship between Okonkwo and Nwoye?

As the students are doing the activity, they appear to understand what is expected of them, and to be comfortable in completing it. Meanwhile, Mr. L. and Ms. R. circulate among the groups and ask clarifying and extension questions (e.g., "When you 'affect' someone, what does that mean? Do you know the story of Abraham?") and answer student questions. The students are busily discussing questions and asking each other where evidence is located.

Student: I think he [Nwoye] feels bad and maybe like he goes a little crazy.
Ms. R.: Where does it say that?

The student looks through text.

Student: Here. "Nwoye knew that Ikemefuna had been killed, and something seemed to give way inside him, like snapping of a tightened bow."

After the students are finished with their tasks, the teachers direct each group to present their answers and evidence to the whole class. One spokesperson from each group takes a turn talking. The other students are expected to take notes on each of the answers. Ms. R. takes the lead for this portion, with Mr. L. providing support.

Student: Nwoye has changed the way he acts because now he wants to be more manly. He kinda acts more like a man.
Ms. R.: What do you think caused this change?
Student: His father. 'Cause he wants to please him but he's also afraid of him.
Ms. R.: What is your support?
Student: It says Okonkwo was inwardly pleased at his son's development, and he knew it was due to Ikemefuna.

Ms. R. then points out where the student is making an important point, but asks for more evidence of his fear.

Ms. R.: Yes, he was afraid of him and wants to please him. How do we know he's afraid? Where is the support?

The student then points to a passage that supports this answer. She also asks her fellow students if they want to add something else to that. A student from another group then asks a clarifying question. Ms. R., satisfied with the student's answer, moves on to the next group's answer. She prefaces the questions, making an explicit reference to the literary term.

> *Ms. R.:* Actually this is a Biblical allusion, guys.

The next student then explains what she's going to do.

> *Student:* Today we will present the differences and similarities between the story of . . .

Following each group's presentation, Ms. R. repeats an important point that the reporting student makes about these two texts, and Mr. L. asks for a quick summary of what was said. The student easily summarizes the group's main points. Mr. L. then extends students' learning: "An allegory is when you can connect something in this story to another story or text. What happens in the Bible story?" In responding, students then talk about the story of Abraham and Isaac.

> *Mr. L.:* What do you think about Okonkwo killing his son?
> *Student:* You can think of it like [. . .]
> *Mr. L.:* Any other questions?
> *Student:* I wanted to say that maybe it's his fear that is dominating him because he's afraid of appearing weak.

In the vignette above, the teachers used questioning to externalize student thinking and assess student understanding. For example, when a student was talking about the changes that Nwoye had experienced, Ms. R. asked the student what she thought caused those changes. This question allowed the student to externalize the inferences she made about the character to gain a deeper understanding of his behaviors. Ms. R.'s next question encouraging the student to offer textual support assessed the student's ability to provide textual evidence for her answers. When the student did not quite understand that Ms. R. was asking for textual evidence of Nwoye's fear and answers with textual evidence to support the father's feelings, Ms. R. praised her for the point and evidence she did provide and then more explicitly rephrased the question for the rest of the class so others would have the opportunity to engage. When Mr. L. asked the group to explain what happened in the Bible story, he was tapping into students' prior knowledge and assessing their understanding of the literary device, the Biblical allusion used in this text. He then explicitly instructed them in the literary term used for this device. The teachers' formative assessment practices, providing multiple entry points for students to engage and use their own words to make meaning of the situation, aided students in simultaneously refining their understanding of the content and of the disciplinary language and practices within the text.

MARBLE HILL HIGH SCHOOL

At Marble Hill High School instruction is focused on a project-based, inquiry approach to learning that is valuable and meaningful for students. Teachers at the school are encouraged to take into consideration each student's "unique gifts, passions, and rights" when designing lessons. There is a powerful conviction among staff members that all students can learn and become successful citizens of society. Diversity of languages and cultures is celebrated at this international school, and a focus on language fluency can be observed throughout classrooms. In this sense, instruction at Marble Hill is engaging and personalized to the needs of every student. (See Appendix C for further information about Marble Hill.)

This school's adoption of the portfolio experience provides an example of a particular form of student assessment. In place since the school's inception, the purpose of the portfolio program has always been to provide multiple means for students to speak meaningfully about what they have learned. This performance-based assessment guides many elements of unit design and lesson planning, as teachers engage in schoolwide practices of project-based learning. Furthermore, curriculum is designed to support these projects by developing cross-subject and cross-grade coherence.

Teachers at Marble Hill are expected to design a variety of project-based learning opportunities for their students. Typically, this form of learning possesses the following characteristics:

- Students working on realistic problems
- Students usually working in pairs or groups
- Students having control over their learning
- Teachers serving as coaches and facilitators (Barron & Darling-Hammond, 2008)

More important, research suggests that when executed effectively, project-based learning can enable students to make gains in "factual learning" that supersede or are equivalent to more traditional methods of instruction (Thomas, 2000). Project-based learning also aims to go beyond the mere development of content knowledge and encourages students to reflect on how they can transfer their skills to new areas.

Students at Marble Hill are required to take part in four projects per year in each class (i.e., two per semester); the numerous opportunities for project-based learning allow students to explore a wide range of topics. In a Global History class, for example, sophomores worked on a Gandhi project that required them to conduct research on India and produce a brochure with their findings. Tenth-graders in a science course participated in a project that involved examining DNA evidence of their teacher's dog and producing articles and a laboratory report on the pet.

All projects generally take up to four weeks to complete, allowing students to pursue a topic in depth. One student noted that the projects are useful because they are preparation for college. The project presentation allows teachers to see projects across disciplinary areas, affording them the opportunity to learn about the practices of their colleagues, share ideas among one another, and become familiar with the diverse needs of students across the school (Barron et al., 1998; Barron & Darling-Hammond, 2008). For ELs, project-based learning is especially beneficial. Projects give students something to "grab onto" as they learn a new language. Through project-based learning, language is used in an authentic way for a specific purpose (Polman & Pea, 2006). Furthermore, since group work is a vital component of many projects, ELs talk to each other and can develop understandings in their home languages as well as create meaning in English.

Although the school has no set format for the structuring of projects, the main goal, according to Assistant Principal Wanda Dingman, is to design lessons that will "get students to use what they know and extend that knowledge to new ideas." Teachers are encouraged to use a school-designed project template with which they can delineate the project objectives, key Common Core standards addressed by the project, guidelines, reflection activities, and scoring rubric for the project.

Much of the work for project-based learning at Marble Hill is done in class. This is especially useful for newcomer or beginner ELs who may not have the resources or know-how to conduct research on their own as they transition into a new school system. As students progress, the work for projects becomes increasingly independent. Furthermore, teachers make sure to identify a set of skills that students should be working toward mastering during the project. Lessons are centered on highlighting the skills that are necessary to complete each task along the way. Since all projects have multiple tasks that build to the final deliverable, teachers collect intermediary work as students move forward with completing the project tasks. This allows teachers to assess student understanding and provide feedback to help students produce a high-quality product.

Since opening its doors back in 2002, Marble Hill has used a system of portfolio presentations to ensure that students have opportunities to engage in deeper learning. Principal Kirsten Larson explained how the decision to implement the portfolio program took into consideration the unique needs of all their students:

Knowing that we were looking at joining [EP] and EL populations in the 50-50 model that [didn't] exist in a very deliberate way and had not existed anywhere else at that time, and knowing the needs of ELs to be able to use language in meaningful ways . . . , we wanted to make sure that our assessment system was rigorous and meaningful and allowed students to be able to show what they were learning and to use language.

Having observed the power of portfolio assessments at other schools, Marble Hill's leaders decided to implement project-based learning "as a way for students to get deeper into content and to have a more extended learning project."

The portfolio assessment program, which is built into the grading policy, provides multiple means for students to reflect and speak about what they have learned throughout the academic year. At Marble Hill, portfolio presentations occur twice a year, every year, for every grade level, and the entire process takes two weeks to organize and complete. Many practices throughout the year prepare students for the presentations. For example, 9th-grade advisory classes help students with presentation skills, and teachers scaffold their lessons to ensure that students master the necessary skills needed for project completion.

The portfolio program has evolved over the years. In a typical semester, students select and present for one hour on one project from every class, totaling six projects, to one staff teacher they have not had during that year. During the presentation, they are expected to present their best work, use language in a meaningful way, reflect on how they have grown, and talk about how each project relates to other subjects.

Since their inception, 12th-grade portfolios have focused on presenting projects and research in a unified way and typically incorporate a discussion about a student's postsecondary goals and educational plans. Recently, Marble Hill has also implemented structured focuses for the lower grades. For example, during the 2013–14 school year, the school added a metacognitive element to the freshmen portfolios, aimed at encouraging students to reflect on *how* they worked to learn the content material. Students were asked to bring their notebooks to the presentation and explain for which class they have had the most success in keeping notes and organizing information. Figure 2.2 provides some examples of questions asked to students that guide their presentations.

In order to streamline the evaluation process, teachers have developed clear guidelines to be used during the student presentations. These guidelines are standardized across the school to ensure that students and teachers are familiar with them prior to the evaluation. The guidelines include information about the project, reflection questions, content questions, prompts, and possible responses. Figure 2.3 includes samples of the type of questions students are asked.

Teachers can use a standard set of reflection questions that are developed schoolwide, but they are strongly encouraged to develop questions of their own to ask students. This shift occurred after considering the Universal Design for Learning framework (see National Center on Universal Design

Figure 2.2. Sample Portfolio Metacognitive Reflective Questions

HUMANITIES

Project Clarification Questions

1. What is a claim? What is a counterclaim?
2. Explain one: Who deserves Jerusalem? Why? Or, do you think Columbus was guilty or innocent? Why?

Course Content Questions

1. What was the Protestant Reformation, and why was it important?
2. How was the Renaissance a turning point in world history?
3. Where were the Mayan, Aztec, and Inca Empires located? Explain how *each* empire adapted to their environments. What kind of scientific advancements did they have?

ENVIRONMENTAL SCIENCE

Project Clarification Questions

1. What does "endangered" mean? Which endangered animal did you study? What are the causes of endangerment? How are we trying to *save* this animal?
2. What is the difference between a direct quote and a paraphrase? In a research paper, how do you write a direct quote versus a paraphrase? Why must all research (direct quotes or paraphrased) be cited?

Course Content Questions

1. What is the difference between **global warming** and **ozone depletion** (the hole in the ozone layer)? You *must* answer this question by discussing: pollutants, human activities that cause each, and impacts of each. Use the diagram to illustrate the relationships across these concepts.

Figure 2.3. Sample Portfolio Reflection Questions

1. How did this project help you understand how humans are affecting biodiversity?
2. Did this project help you improve your *research* skills? Explain.
3. Did this project help you improve your *writing* skills? Explain.
4. What specific steps did you take to complete this project?
5. How did writing this piece make you feel?
6. What was difficult about this project? What was easy?
7. If you did this project again, what would you do differently? Why?

for Learning, 2015), which promotes the adaptation of curriculum for all students by providing multiple means of presentation, action and expression, and engagement.

One distinguishing feature of the portfolio program at Marble Hill is that the final presentations are conducted one student to one teacher, rather than via a panel, as is usually the case in other schools. Part of the reason that the portfolios are presented one-on-one is that students are required to present every semester, and coordinating a panel of community members, school staff, and peer colleagues would have made the incorporation of portfolio assessment more challenging. Additionally, unlike other portfolio programs that are highly student-driven or highly dictated by the staff, Marble Hill developed a program that allows for more back-and-forth between students and teachers. Projects are not entirely student-driven, but students are given a choice about what projects to select and present on. Furthermore, students are encouraged to practice their presentations to one another during Saturday school and receive support from teachers if necessary. Feedback is provided shortly after the presentation so that students can apply the feedback to the future work. In addition to being assessed on presentation, they are also given feedback on their fluency, which is defined as ease and confidence in the subject matter and its presentation. Furthermore, students are assessed on language use, professionalism, and preparedness in their presentations.

Portfolios provide numerous benefits for students. One student commented on the usefulness of the portfolio experience: "I like the fact that every semester there are portfolios at the end. It's a way to practice [for] job interviews." The portfolios also provide an excellent opportunity for teachers and students to get to know each other well, and for teachers to learn more about the diverse linguistic needs of students at the school. For teachers of ELs, it is important that they remain aware of what English Proficient (EP) students are doing and how they are performing. Similarly, teachers of EP students can assess how the EL population is performing. The portfolio evaluations enable teachers to gain context for how students are progressing across the board throughout the school.

As a key feature of Marble Hill's instructional program, the portfolio assessment experience provides meaningful ways for staff to understand student learning and for students to develop their language and content-specific skills.

NEW WORLD HIGH SCHOOL

Drawing on data from standardized assessments, such as the New York State English as a Second Language Achievement Test (NYSESLAT), coupled with a continuous improvement mindset, New World High School incorporates assessment information to guide decisions in ways that tie into the mission and vision of the school (see Appendix C for more information on New World). This school provides an instructive example of the design element component of utilization of assessment data.

New World uses various formal assessments to identify students by English proficiency level and facilitate the allocation of supports. In 9th grade, all incoming students are assessed across content areas and in English proficiency using the NYSESLAT and the Language Assessment Battery-Revised (LAB-R) exam. Based on the results of these assessments, students are identified as belonging to five "ESL levels":

1. Newcomers and beginners
2. Low and intermediate
3. High intermediate and advanced
4. Advanced ready for English
5. English Language Arts

Similar levels are used in math, science, and social studies. Students are identified by ESL level to facilitate the allocation of supports.

However, students may only be identified temporarily with an initial English proficiency level. Teachers are constantly reassessing student placements and administering other forms of assessments throughout the school year to ensure that students are receiving the most rigorous academic program. Cases in which students are reassigned after several months are commonplace. For example, students with strong English acquisition skills may have improved their language skills sufficiently to move to another level within three to four months, or students with strong math skills may require a change in schedule halfway through the year. Assistant Principal Mithat Gashi noted, "Generally, these are students who have a strong background in their native language . . . [so] their teachers recommend to move them up." The decision to move students to a different English proficiency level, however, is a collective process—one that is taken very seriously by a student's teachers (both current and future) as well as administrators. As Principal Salazar explained:

> Even after [initial designations], we meet with the teachers to ask, "How is this working out?" and we make adjustments, so we look at multiple things. Every term, we sit together to see which kids can be moved. This [decision is made] not just with the ESL teachers. . . . The entire team has to agree to move a student.

In order to demonstrate the necessity of a placement shift and to design the best academic schedule for a student, teachers and administrators use the most up-to-date information, including classroom observations, student work, writing samples, grades, and formative and summative assessments.

Within a class, it is possible that there will be students with various language abilities. Principal Salazar commented on the diversity of proficiency levels within classrooms: "In each block, we have different levels, but not too far apart. You can't have in the same class kids that are close to proficient and at the same time kids who have just arrived to this country." Strategies to support students therefore vary based on ESL level: the more basic the level, the stronger the scaffolding. As students progress through their program, the aim is to remove most (although not all) of the scaffolds. Teachers use frequent formative and summative assessments to monitor student learning. One teacher said, "We test all the time . . . midterms, final assessments." Teachers additionally use methods like quick writes, exit slips, and follow-up questions. One teacher shared, "I also ask students to develop their own 'how' or 'why' questions—and you can immediately tell whether they are on a superficial level or a deeper level."

This continuous assessment is done with the intent of ensuring that all students are grasping class concepts—teachers typically do not move on until students understand the material. Summative assessments give teachers the opportunity to determine whether student learning has occurred after a set time, which is useful for monitoring progress toward proficiency in set standards. Meanwhile, the practice of consistently administering formative assessments is especially relevant for enhancing teaching practices to increase student learning. As ELs face the demands of learning content and language simultaneously, it is important for their teachers to detect misunderstandings early on to ensure that they can provide the appropriate supports (Alvarez, Ananada, Walqui, Sato, & Rabinowitz, 2014).

The following classroom vignette provides an example of how a teacher, Ms. T., structured a lesson first to establish student understanding of historical facts and then to provide a unique opportunity for students to showcase their learning of the information, allowing the teacher to formatively assess their progress.

In a 10th-grade Global Studies class, 20 ELs sit in small groups of five. Ms. T. begins class by asking students to reflect on their homework and what they accomplished yesterday. One student raises his hand to recap the lesson from the previous day: "We learned about the problems that Italy was going through during the 1920s and 1930s." On the whiteboard, the lesson objective for the day is written clearly: "How did dictators rise to power in the 1920s and 1930s?" Ms. T. asks a student to read the goal out loud to the entire class, and then switches modes to explain the purpose of the assignment.

Today students will write a diary entry from the perspective of Italian citizens living during the time of Mussolini's regime. The entry must include a historically accurate description of the issues faced by Italian citizens at this time, a description of a fictional citizen, and an explanation of their fictional citizen's opinion.

During this period of whole-group discussion, Ms. T. offers an example of a diary entry by sharing some model text. She also encourages students to think critically about how they will write their entry before they break out into small-group discussion. She asks, "Do I support or oppose Mussolini?" And she follows up with, "What does 'oppose' mean?" She additionally helps students recall previously learned information by asking them to brainstorm possible challenges faced by Italian citizens during that time: "What were some of the issues? Go back to your reading if you don't remember." She checks for understanding before proceeding: "What did Mussolini want for women?" On a document camera, a graphic organizer is displayed. It contains attributes of dictator Benito Mussolini—the country and political system he represents, the government he replaced, and his ideology. Once students create a fictional citizen to write about, they then have to go back to the readings to look for connections that would be relevant to that citizen. Ms. T. shares underlined text from her reading as an example.

Students open up their notebooks and readings from prior days. These documents are heavily annotated with information to help them understand the text. As the class transitions to independent or small-group work, students are given the choice to work individually or with their peers. Ms. T. circulates around the room reviewing assignments while students begin their work to find evidence to support the fictional citizens' opinions of Mussolini.

Evident in this example are the numerous ways in which the teacher scaffolds the content to make sure that all students are comprehending the task at hand. Also notable is the way that Ms. T. structures the lesson to allow students to demonstrate their understanding of historical facts as well as how language is used in the text in varied ways. Before students begin work on their own, she reviews historical facts about Mussolini's regime by asking questions that prompt students to refresh their knowledge of previous lessons. She defines academic words embedded in the texts, shares graphic organizers with key information, and guides students in understanding the form and structure of a diary entry in historical writing.

Her objective is to ensure that students understand the historical context before they begin to work on their own, and she gauges their initial level of understanding through conversation. Ms. T. assesses student learning in a deeper way, however, through the actual exercise, which requires students to write a historically accurate diary entry from the perspective of a fictional citizen. In this way, students integrate historical facts creatively while making explanations and arguments backed up with evidence. This type of assessment is particularly helpful for ELs, as researchers have suggested that in order to foster a student's ability to make sense of complex text, "ELs may be well served by opportunities to explore—and justify—their own 'textual hypotheses,' even if their initial interpretations diverge from those of the teacher" (Bunch, Kibler, & Pimentel, 2012, p. 5).

CONCLUSION

Thoughtful and detailed assessment strategies are an important design principle in several of the case study schools. Assessment practices in these schools are both formative and summative and take place consistently throughout the academic year. Qualitatively, these practices can be said to demonstrate a continuous improvement mindset, varied forms of assessment practices, and the utilization of assessment data.

A continuous improvement mindset refers to the ongoing expectation that all students can and will improve. At Dual Language, for example, teachers adjust formative assessment practices to take students' developing English proficiency into account. At ITAVA, teachers were found to employ thoughtful, text-based questions during discussions to help students clarify and provide evidence for their thinking and to stretch their understanding. Varied forms of assessment practices are exemplified in the portfolio-based approach to student learning at Marble Hill, where project-based learning is the focus of student instruction. Students work to prepare for one portfolio presentation in each subject twice per year. Because all projects have multiple tasks that build to the final project, there are multiple opportunities to provide students with feedback throughout the term. The utilization of assessment data is best reflected by New World's use of multiple assessments—many formative in nature—to reassess students' placements. This is especially true as students progress quickly in their English proficiency and are moved on to the next level.

The next chapter highlights yet another design principle of successful high schools for ELs—the intensive social-emotional supports provided to students.

CHAPTER 3

Design Element 3
Intensive Social-Emotional Support

> One who cares must meet the cared-for just as he or she is, as a whole human being with individual needs and interests. (Noddings, 2012, p. 109)

The design elements discussed in the first two chapters focused on the academic aspects of effective schooling for ELs. In this chapter, we turn to the nonacademic but critical design element of the intensive social-emotional supports that can enable ELs to achieve academic success (Durlak, Weissberg, Dymnicki, Taylor, & Schellinger, 2011). At the schools we studied, students are supported to develop the following traits, skills, behaviors, and attitudes: self-awareness, self-management, social awareness, perseverance, mindsets, learning strategies, responsible decisionmaking, and social and relational skills. These have been referred to as the "non-cognitive factors" influencing school success (Farrington et al., 2012).

The effectiveness of social-emotional supports is founded on an understanding of students' diverse histories, enduring relationships of trust across the school community, the availability of wraparound counseling and family supports, and an unwavering attention and care to the "whole child" (Hamedani & Darling-Hammond, 2014; Noddings, 2015).

At the schools we studied, social-emotional support starts as soon as a student enrolls. The staff welcomes families in from day one and shows them the support system in place for their children. This immediate attention to students' backgrounds establishes a foundation of trust that is the basis for future communication and involvement. Because many staff members share their students' experience as immigrants and ELs, staff members empathize deeply with their students' challenges as they navigate their schooling. This respect for students' experiences, and the realization that students often need additional supports in navigating life in a new country, allow teachers and counselors at these schools to build relationships of care and trust with their students.

Beyond getting to know their students, these schools sustain their social-emotional support of students through close counseling from adults, either through structured advisory programs or mentoring relationships. The schools also go above and beyond in connecting students and their families with wraparound services related to health, housing, food security, employment, and community resources so that immigrant students and their families transition successfully into their new communities.

Finally, students are not only pushed to succeed academically, but are guided in their whole development through systematic attention to their social-emotional well-being and skills to ensure that they thrive both academically and personally in high school and beyond. As a result of the nurturing, supportive environment at these schools, students view their schools as places of refuge, and the school community as an extension of their own family.

This design element of intensive social-emotional support includes the following essential components:

- *Integrated Social and Emotional Supports for Success.* School teams have deep understanding that academic and social-emotional learning for students work in symbiotic ways in promoting student engagement in learning and postsecondary outcomes (National Research Council, 2012).
- *School Policies and Practices to Promote Social-Emotional Well-Being.* Schoolwide practices and policies attend to students' social-emotional well-being (e.g., intake interviews, home visits, advisory programs, counseling, and mental health services).
- *Collaboration with Community Partners.* Full-service community schools provide wraparound services for families in need and their students (e.g., newcomers and SIFE).

To demonstrate how the components of this design element are implemented, we present five examples of schools that are organized with full-service wraparound supports for students and families, along with the ways school teams are building trust and independence for their students through systematic attention to the needs of the whole child.

BOSTON INTERNATIONAL HIGH SCHOOL AND NEWCOMERS ACADEMY

When asked about the students at BINcA, a guidance counselor describes her students with admiration:

Our kids are fearless. You have kids that crossed the border and in two weeks found their way to the East Coast . . . and come to school every day, go to work, get out at one o'clock in the morning from a restaurant, and still make it back here on time and are doing homework . . . They're coming, and they're graduating, and they're going off to college.

This understanding of who their students are and the experiences that have shaped them is an important basis for the strong relationships that staff members have built with their students.

Integrated Social and Emotional Supports for Success

Starting with the initial intake interview that BINcA has with each student and family in their home language, the school team builds knowledge and understanding of the student's personal and academic history in planning the necessary supports and services that will help the student succeed in this new environment. Sample questions from the student intake interview can be seen in Figure 3.1.

The instructional team and support staff at BINcA are guided by the "4 Cs," representing "Connection, Communication, Collaboration, and Creativity." Classroom discussions, hallway banter, and guidance sessions with students are influenced by connections to students' past experiences

Figure 3.1. Sample Student Intake Interview Questions

PERSONAL HISTORY

1. What language(s) do you speak at home?
2. Where were you born? (City/Country)
3. When did you arrive to the United States? (Month/Year)
4. Where did you live before entering the United States?
5. Did you live anywhere else in the United States before you came to Boston?
6. When did you arrive in Boston?
7. With whom do you live?

SCHOOLING AND ACADEMIC HISTORY

1. In what language(s) do you feel most comfortable reading and writing?
2. How old were you when you began the first grade/primary school?
3. What language(s) did teachers use with you when you were going to school in your country?
4. How did you get to school? How long did it take you to get to school each time you went to school?
5. Did you go to school every day, or did you miss days? Why did you miss school days?
6. How many students were in each of your classes?
7. How long were your classes? How many minutes?
8. What subjects did you study in school?
9. Have you ever been in a special needs program, or have you received special needs services? Please indicate types of programs or services.
10. What are your interests? (e.g., music, arts, theater, etc.)

and histories as Latino, Cape Verdean, or Haitian youths. As the Dean of Discipline explained, "The outreach and trust-building often surprises students." This attentiveness makes students feel cared for and reduces the external anxieties that may impact students' experiences at BINcA, and ultimately enables the school to function peacefully. The support staff works closely with the instructional staff to understand the various modes of expressions (e.g., theater, music, arts), passions, and creativity that can further students' long-term educational goals.

School Policies and Practices to Promote Social-Emotional Well-Being

Knowing that many of their students have faced trauma and upheaval in their recent transitions to the United States, staff members at BINcA believe it is extremely important to create stability for their students from day one. They do this formally through an extensive array of wraparound services designed to meet individual students' needs, and informally through the constant expression of care and support. The following vignette illustrates how the school supports newly arrived immigrant students with sensitivity and care:

Audrey, a 16-year-old Haitian native, recently immigrated to the Dorchester area of Boston to live with her distant relatives who work in the service industry. After taking a language placement test administered by the district office, the district liaison recommended that Audrey be placed at BINcA because of its diversity and supports for ELs.

Audrey and her aunt arrive at BINcA with some information from the district office about the schooling process but limited knowledge about BINcA and its specific offerings. At their first meeting, Audrey and her aunt describe to the guidance counselor Audrey's journey to America, her experiences in education back in Haiti, and her thoughts and aspirations at BINcA. During this time, the counselor moves fluidly between English and Haitian Creole and steers the conversation toward some of the questions from the intake interview (refer to Figure 3.1). Within this one-hour conversation, the counselor notes particular strengths and needs of Audrey and her family and uses this opportunity to garner their trust as they begin this educational journey together as partners.

During the first two weeks of Audrey's enrollment, the counselor greets Audrey and informally checks in with her in the hallways and before and after school to make sure her transition to BINcA has been smooth. Formally, she checks in with Audrey at the two-week mark, as she does with many incoming students, and makes sure Audrey has an adult figure to turn to and to troubleshoot any unanticipated needs that haven't been met. At this two-week check-in, the counselor inquiries about a student's home life and general health (e.g., physical, mental, emotional), as well as food and safety concerns that a student may have in her new country. This type of conversation will continue until and beyond graduation day. Of course, the discussions will move from this important transitional and adjustment period toward exploring and setting the groundwork for future opportunities after graduation.

The vignette about Audrey exemplifies the intentional ways in which the BINcA team builds relationships and trust with students and their families. In addition to the care provided through the intake process and the provision of resources and services, BINcA also safeguards the well-being of its students through many informal practices on the part of adults on campus. During passing periods, the headmaster chats with teachers and students, taking the pulse of the school. During lunch time, former Headmaster Nicole Bahnam conversed with students, shared stories, shared lunch with them, and observed the social interactions among her students. She believes that lunch is a critical time to assess how students are adjusting socially to the school. By observing who they are sitting with, she could get a sense of how well students were fitting in and whether they needed additional social supports.

The effectiveness of the staff's supportive practices is evident in the comments of Flora, whose son Alex is a rising junior. She recounted her son's first days as a new student at BINcA who did not know any English:

My son Alex came [to the United States] in September 2013 and was scared to come to this new school [BINcA]. He didn't know any English and wasn't sure how he would express himself or communicate. When he came home from the first day, I was worried, but he said that it was the "best day" for him. He told me that someone took care of him, and teachers ate lunch with him so he wouldn't be eating alone and made him feel comfortable in this new place and immediately my son felt like it was the best school. First impressions mattered, and it was very good. For me, the teachers made my son feel comfortable, and communicated with me, explaining problems and successes. I feel like this is the right place for my son.

These positive first impressions served as small stepping-stones toward building student trust and commitment toward schooling. Alex's mother further explained how her son feels like he is part of a family:

I can see that my son is enthusiastic, likes to learn, likes to come to school, and feels like part of a community. Over time, my son has been able to communicate and work with others, and they get together and are part of each other's lives. The teachers understand . . . and work together as a group—this is one of the things that contributes to their success.

Care and consideration for the whole child also characterize the disciplinary system at BINcA. The philosophy of former Headmaster Bahnam is that a safe school environment is the number-one priority for learning. As she put it, it is important for students to feel "included and cared for; they need a place with structure to help them grow, not a thousand small rules that govern their behavior." She reminded teachers that their students have different profiles and histories, and that being patient is part of the teachers' job. She believes that 50% of what the school provides needs to be social-emotional support—helping students to feel wanted and to believe in themselves. As students settle into their lives in the United States, their emotional needs will stabilize, and they will thrive academically as well.

In keeping with this philosophy, behavior management at the school focuses on conflict resolution and student communication. Because staff members know that conflicts among students can escalate quickly if students do not understand why others are aggressive toward them, translation and mediation are used to resolve conflicts. The support staff organizes opportunities to help students examine their choices and acts as "coaches" in guiding students toward alternative ways to resolve conflicts. By emphasizing a problem-solving mindset rather than the punitive aspects of discipline, staff members at BINcA maintain a safe campus environment while preserving the social-emotional health of their students.

In our conversation with a district leader, she described BINcA's approach toward conflict management among their diverse student populations:

> The staff and leadership are incredibly attentive to students' social, emotional, and physical health—which they see as critical to learning. Diversity here is a strength and the team is proactive in giving students tools toward conflict resolution that help students understand each other's cultures and religion—because at times, their views and opinions differ. The time after the 2013 Boston Marathon bombing was tense across our schools, especially for those who served Muslim students. The team at BINcA foresaw this fear and quickly moved to put a plan in place. They designed lessons to help students understand why cultures and religions can clash.

After the bombing incident, the BINcA staff worked proactively and used culturally sensitive methods to stimulate reflection and dialogue among their students. They anticipated and de-escalated potential conflicts and negative stereotyping after the tragedy that befell the larger Boston community.

Collaboration with Community Partners

The counseling team members, all from immigrant families themselves, see their work as being both community-builders as well as advocates for families, assessing the children's and families' needs, and getting the right services and resources that support student and family success in this new country. BINcA's school dean explains that the school and family support team is well-connected with the local community and service providers:

> We're able to provide students and their families with access to much-needed resources such as food stamps or housing—having that connection with people who have those resources is a big plus . . . We're going beyond just the child's education. We're helping their family.

Students realize that their teachers care about more than just their education, and this fills them with pride and respect for their school. Some students and families see the BINcA community as "an extension of their family." The guidance counselor reiterated the importance of welcoming families to the school from day one. Showing families the support system that is in place for their children builds a foundation of trust that is the basis for future communication and involvement.

It is this nurturing family-like environment that allows the students at BINcA to feel welcomed from day one and thrive in classrooms that embrace and acknowledge the histories and strengths of each student, and brings them together in a close-knit learning community from early adolescence into adulthood.

HIGH SCHOOL FOR DUAL LANGUAGE AND ASIAN STUDIES

From the moment potential students are matched to the school in the spring all the way to the start of the school year, the leadership and guidance teams at Dual Language work together in planning out the academic and college preparatory program that best suits the needs of the incoming and current student body. The teams consider both in-school time as well as out-of-school time (after school, weekends, and summers) to be critical developmental and growth periods for their students. As a result, the teams focus a considerable amount of attention on planning the types of courses that best suit the academic and linguistic needs of students and figuring out how to tailor learning experiences so that students will graduate from Dual Language prepared to be successful in their postsecondary lives.

Integrated Social and Emotional Supports for Success

When asked about school practices or strategies that undergird the school's theory of action for ELs, Principal Li Yan explained:

We have 23% ELs, but if you look, 80% of our students are former ELs. We don't have any programs specifically. We have multiple levels for ESL courses, so that students have enough contact within 45-minute classes. Kids can test out of the ESL program, but that doesn't mean they are proficient. We give the students ESL support for all four years. Most ESL students have three periods of English for four years. You have to look at what their needs are. Everyone takes the writing class here, a college writing class. We started that for ELs. We also use the English Regents goal of 65–75, and we make all students take the college writing class.

As described by Principal Yan, the school focuses the programming based on student needs, sets high and achievable goals for their ELs, and provides the necessary support for students to be successful in their coursework. Courses vary year-to-year based on the growth and achievement of the students. The guidance team takes note of all incoming students' academic records in the spring, along with their scores on a language proficiency test given by the school, and designs courses that can meet the students' needs.

Students begin the college-going process at the start of their freshman year when they are introduced to the guidance team and begin to talk about the opportunities that are available for students over their course of their academic careers at Dual Language. The strength of the relationships that the guidance team has built with students can be seen in the perpetual buzz of students who congregate in and outside of the guidance offices. There is a mutual respect between the students and the guidance team because the guidance team approaches each student holistically, garners student trust, and anticipates situations before they grow to be more difficult problems.

During students' sophomore and junior years, students meet with the guidance team in small groups of four during the school year (even on Saturdays) to set goals, plan action items needed for the college application process, share concerns and questions, and check in on progress toward college-going goals. By senior year, students are working with the counseling team on a one-on-one basis, planning campus visits, completing applications, writing and editing essays, prepping for interviews, making sense of acceptance packages, selecting the right school, and communicating the college transition to families. Serena, an alumna we interviewed who is now at a local college, recalls her senior year experiences in preparing for college:

I remember in September of my senior year, we would get links to different college programs. The college team took us to college campuses. They highly encouraged us to visit schools even though it may not be a right fit. I found that to be useful. They found different links and sights for us to see and learn more about the world. If I just Googled it myself, I would see pictures that are online but I wouldn't see the real [picture] of what the life is.

The guidance team works tirelessly to give students realistic expectations of what college is like and connect students' high school experiences with the continued rigor that exists in college life. Because many of these students are the first in their family to attend college, the school makes sure that its graduates have realistic and ambitious aspirations so that they are prepared to enter and succeed on their own in college.

School Policies and Practices to Promote Social-Emotional Well-Being

The school has heavily invested in staffing its student support services for their 416 students (2014–15 figures). They fund for two full-time and one half-time guidance counselor as well as one full-time college counselor. Additionally, Assistant Principal Miriam Uzzan leads and teaches college preparatory courses on Saturdays for juniors and seniors. In this work, Uzzan spends time learning about students' strengths and goals as they prepare their college applications. In turn, she uses knowledge about the students' goals, aspirations, and needs to bolster how the teaching and guidance staff supports students toward college and career readiness. This additional time and course structure on Saturday mornings, together with the high ratio of counseling and college support staff members to students, allows a tremendous level of individual attention to students and their families. For example, the guidance team shared a student's recent experience as a new arrival from China:

We had a student that was coming in late, and we noticed the change of his demeanor. [When] we started counseling him, we realized he was dealing with a lot of stuff. His mom was in China, and his dad works 18 hours a day. He was lonely, not fitting in, probably wanting to go back to China. Even [after] just a few weeks of counseling, he was totally transformed. Really watching the little things, the little signs that things are not [going] right, is really to know the students.

This description from the guidance team is not atypical of the range of students, especially ELs, who are at Dual Language. Often students were born in the United States and sent back to China to live with relatives, then returned to the United States to finish high school. Other students travel by themselves and live with relatives or guardians, or have parents or caregivers who work two daily shifts in addition to weekends to support their family. Fostering a sense of trust among students takes time and patience for students and staff members.

By embracing and acknowledging the histories and strengths of each student, Dual Language has created a family-like environment that allows the students to thrive academically and emotionally.

IT TAKES A VILLAGE ACADEMY

The student-centered approach to education at It Takes A Village Academy maximizes student engagement and learning. This approach is particularly successful with ELs, whose educational needs are highly individual and complex because those students are learning not only academic content but also how to use a new language and often how to navigate a new society and culture. Student-centeredness is observable in every facet of this school's structures, policies, and practices, and the student support systems in place at ITAVA are a notable illustration of this underlying mindset.

ITAVA staff understands that sustained and integrated social-emotional learning helps to engage students, build trust, foster community, and improve achievement. Many ITAVA students face tough challenges inside and outside the school walls. Addressing social-emotional needs is essential to their academic success, and is a heavy focus of students' advisory period. The staff is heavily focused on improving students' skills in self-management, responsible decisionmaking, self- and social-awareness, and relationships. The school also works hard to provide supportive, caring, and trained staff members who are readily available to meet with students and offer guidance, whether during advisory or in the offices of the guidance counselors and other administrators. As one of ITAVA's community partners noted, "Every single student in this building is known by almost every single teacher." This responsiveness strengthens students' connectedness to school. Teachers report that students see the school as a place of refuge. As one staff member put it, "We have to kick them out at night. They don't want to leave."

Students are offered emotional support through a well-developed and effective advisory program at ITAVA, with a student-to-teacher ratio of 10-to-1. Upon enrollment, students are assigned to an advisory teacher for the remainder of their high school careers. That advisor supports their social-emotional needs and can act as an advocate for struggling students with their teachers. As one counselor explained:

> The advisor has that close-knit relationship with that student. We don't look at it as a teaching period, as it's more or less a roundtable, more informal, getting to know the student. It's important to have the student have an adult to go to if you have an issue. To have this one person, and to build that relationship with that one person. . . .
> You need to address the social-emotional issues. It's not just about academics, but about the whole child.

Students' positive academic outcomes at ITAVA may partially be attributed to personalized relationships with the advisors and to the trust that the students place in their academic mentors, which allows the adults to intervene or provide support and access to resources where necessary. Based on our interviews with mentors and students, we suspect that these relationships play a significant role in motivating students to take on the challenges of a college-ready curriculum.

MANHATTAN BRIDGES HIGH SCHOOL

The adults at Manhattan Bridges view social-emotional support as a crucial part of what they do, and therefore it is integrated thoughtfully throughout their work. The school recognizes the needs of the whole child and gives systematic attention to students' social and emotional well-being and skills—such as coping with failure, stress control, realistic and adaptive goal-setting, planning, decisionmaking, and motivation—to ensure that they thrive academically and personally in this environment and beyond. The approach is not limited to any one or two models, and the school's policies and practices incorporate multiple organic and interwoven strategies.

The counseling and support staff play an important role in providing social-emotional support for students. If students are having a hard time adjusting to the school, one of the three counselors has lunch with those students to figure out what can be done to make the school environment better for them. Despite their workloads of supporting over 500 students, the counselors work hard to talk to all students and get to know them on a personal level. They communicate closely with students' teachers, collaborating with them if a student has a hardship or will be absent for a long time. The counseling staff also works to ensure that students feel connected to their home environment and culture, collaborating with institutions like the Puerto Rican Family Institute to provide extra support. As another layer of support, a dedicated attendance coordinator monitors students' absences and investigates if students are absent for three or more days, often conducting home visits to gain a better understanding of a student's situation.

The school takes a flexible, team approach to supporting the social and emotional needs of students, which helps students view Manhattan Bridges as a second home and an extension of their family. A youth development team comprised of teachers, guidance counselors, and a parent coordinator also works to ensure that students' voices are always heard. The team solicits feedback from students, examines student progress, and works closely with family members to surface student concerns and improve the student experience. Having consciously built a caring and nurturing environment for their students, the staff quickly notes if something is wrong and works as a team to provide support. For example, when one of Ms. G.'s students was coming late to class every day, she grew increasingly concerned. And when the student finally confided in the teacher that she was late because she needed to take her little sister to school in the morning, Ms. G. arranged a meeting with the student, her mom, and her counselor. During the meeting, Ms. G. and the counselor let the student and her mom know that she is a strong and talented student, and that Ms. G. would work with her to make sure she still masters all the material in the class, despite being half an hour late each day. Ms. G. and the counselor demonstrated their understanding that the family is juggling many responsibilities, and stepped up to do whatever it would take to support the student. At the end of the meeting, the student was overwhelmed with emotion by the knowledge that her teachers understood her family obligations and were willing to work with her to help her succeed.

The school's efforts toward building student confidence and resilience constitute intentional and meaningful work that is integrated not just in the support services but also within classrooms. Classes incorporate numerous activities that help build social-emotional skills. Teachers foster an atmosphere of respect and safety among students within their classrooms, emphasizing their shared experiences as English learners and reminding them that they are there to help one another. Teachers also work hard to connect and build relationships with students. As a result, students feel welcomed by their teachers and classmates and are not afraid to make mistakes in class. As one student emphasized, "[Teachers are] willing to teach you and make you feel comfortable. Then you're not afraid of doing things that many other people won't." In the supportive environment that is part of the school culture at Manhattan Bridges, teachers do not just view themselves as teachers of subjects, but rather of young people with individual needs and aspirations. Teachers work closely with the support staff to lower the barriers to students' paths to success. Students, in turn, trust that the adults on campus have their best interests in mind and feel acknowledged and supported in meeting the high expectations of the school.

Assistant Principal George Lock also discussed how the social-emotional support at Manhattan Bridges includes a focus on life skills. He said, "Manhattan Bridges goes further by helping kids learn to avoid failure." The school gives students strategies to help with organization, metacognition, goal-setting, and self-expression, and to help them believe in their future, achieve the college and career goals they set for themselves, overcome the obstacles they may face in life, and hold themselves personally responsible for reaching their objectives. Every problem is used as a learning opportunity. For instance, if a student has an issue with a teacher, the school helps the student resolve it and then points out how the skills involved will be useful in college when dealing with professors. The goal is to build students' personal life skills "toolbox" so that students can use their tools when they confront difficult situations. Principal Mirza Sanchez-Medina shared:

We are looking at access all the time. Our job really is to look for ways to take roadblocks out and have [the students] walk . . . I'm not going to carry the child. I'm going to teach them how to walk and develop that process so that they can say, "I feel confident." But, if you fall, we will be here to pick you up.

Even in the face of the tremendous challenges these inner-city youths face, Manhattan Bridges sees its individual students thriving increasingly over time and succeeding in college and careers as a result of all the school's concerted work toward social-emotional support and youth development.

MARBLE HILL HIGH SCHOOL

At Marble Hill, support and relationship-building for students and their families start at enrollment and intake. The enrollment and intake process involves a variety of assessments to ensure that the student is placed into the appropriate courses and program. Assistant Principal Wanda Dingman discussed the intake procedure in further detail:

The Home Language Survey [is administered] to see if the student should be tested for ESL. We try to do it immediately before they even have a schedule, because if you don't [test immediately] you are creating a schedule that is not even appropriate for the student. Another big part of this for us is that we have a very, very big SIFE population. We [also] have a lot of students who come from middle school who are *incorrectly* identified as SIFE, so there is a lot of work that goes into that as well.

By identifying the academic and social-emotional needs of the students upon arrival, the school designs individualized programs that best fit their needs, and targeted support is administered immediately.

Recognizing that the high school transition may be challenging, especially for ELs who are new to the country, Marble Hill invites enrolled students to attend a Summer Bridge program aimed at building skills such as note-taking and basic reading and writing. Referral services are also offered at the school. Students receive services such as physical examinations, immunizations, and mental health and vision services through the School-Based Health Center and Center for Community Health and Education located on the first floor of the campus. Community partners, like Changing the Odds, a youth development project offered by the Morris Heights Health Center, also support the needs of Marble Hill students. One staff member commented on the need for these services and the social-emotional challenges faced by some of their students:

Students come from various different countries . . . [and] there's an adjustment period. I experienced it myself coming here at the age of thirteen. We try to make the students understand that, yes, we understand this is a different way of living for you. And we try to guide them. . . . We are lucky to say we have a school-based clinic in the building with two child psychologists, so we use their services a lot. It's very helpful, because a lot of times our students come here and leave their families behind, whether it is one parent or both of them. So, it's not always just about an adjustment period. It's coming here with half of your family staying back home. That is something that takes a toll on our kids, and a lot of times they don't know how to deal with it. They need the liaison in between them to help them navigate.

The case of a small group of Yemeni boys who arrived in the 2014–15 school year illustrates how Marble Hill provides targeted social-emotional and academic services to support ELs. These SIFE students were placed into the ESL program strand for newcomers, SIFE, and beginner ELs, which is geared toward establishing basic communication skills, and gives special attention to SIFE. These students were grouped together so that they could support one another in their primary language. They were also given additional supports, such as small-group skill classes (e.g., numeracy or computer and typing classes), book clubs that use engaging texts to support literacy, lunch groups with counselors and teachers, access to the SIFE library (which includes low-level/high-interest books for small-group or individual use), and participation in the Explorers Club (which gives students an opportunity to go on weekend field trips to various cultural institutions in New York City), as well as Saturday school. Assistant Principal Dingman described the services for SIFE students:

We did get a SIFE grant, and we are really trying to get programs up and running for these kids. The thing that we do is we have mentoring after school, five kids to one teacher, based on what their [needs] are. So if it is a literacy issue we move those super-low [-literacy] kids together with someone who is well-versed in helping them. A lot of times we are expecting them to do Regents-level work, but they really have a gap. So [we are] trying to fill that gap, while still trying to keep them afloat in school, working after school and on Saturdays to fill in the gap.

Although there is no "typical" day for a SIFE student, Marble Hill generally provides them with multiple supports. Much like newcomer and beginner ELs, they are placed in a double-period English class to promote literacy and to foster deeper relationships of trust with teachers. Because

Marble Hill individualizes programming, however, interventions and programs may vary by student. Those who need the most support may have a different set of weekly activities than students who are more advanced. The school leader's belief in working with the "whole child" sets the tone for how other staff members approach their work with individual students. In these ways, Marble Hill prioritizes social-emotional support in service of academic success.

CONCLUSION

Social-emotional supports for students and their families figure prominently in the success of these schools. It begins as soon as students enroll. Caring for the whole child is evident in the ways in which schools provide families with access to resources that mitigate issues related to housing, health, employment, and food insecurity. Observed key components of providing for the social-emotional needs of students consist of: (1) integrated social and emotional supports for success, (2) school practices and policies that attend to students' emotional well-being, and (3) collaboration with community partners. Examples of such supports, while abundant, are summarized below.

Manhattan Bridges recognizes the interconnectedness of students' academic, social, and emotional lives and equips students with strategies to improve organization, metacognition, goal-setting, and self-expression, all the while encouraging students to believe that their life goals can be achieved. Teachers focus on their students' individual needs and aspirations. BINcA is similarly engaged in attending to students' emotional well-being. Among the practices and policies in place for supporting students is a well-implemented and effective advisory program that pairs each student with a teacher advisor who can support their social-emotional needs throughout their time at the school and advocate on their behalf. Despite the difficult circumstances in which many of these students live, students at BINcA have come to regard their school as a place of refuge and safety. And yet the job of tending to students' social and emotional well-being cannot be accomplished alone. As is the case with other schools, Marble Hill works with a variety of community partners, like Changing the Odds, a youth development project offered by the Morris Heights Health Center in New York City, which supports the social-emotional needs of students, many of whom are adjusting to a new culture without the comforts of the life they once knew.

In the next chapter, we focus on the fourth design element: the unique characteristics of the talented professionals who ably lead each school.

CHAPTER 4

Design Element 4

Passionate, Strategic, and Mission-Driven Leadership

> I'd like to mention one thing that is very emblematic of [New World's]
> success. I think leadership is everything. . . . I don't think you can have an
> outstanding school without a great *leader*, and in this case you have a great
> leadership *team*. (a community partner)

Fiercely dedicated, highly organized, and strategic leaders are essential if schools are to implement the design elements discussed in Chapters 1–3 and fulfill the promise of ELs' success. The leaders of the schools we studied are visionary and innovative, and think outside the box in designing learning specifically for ELs. Across these schools, the leaders leave no stone unturned in meticulously planning every aspect of the school experience to drive success for ELs. Failure to fulfill their EL mission is not an option.

Leaders in these schools serve multiple and varied roles. The type of passionate, strategic, and mission-driven leadership we observed in action can be described as a blend of transformational, distributed, and instructional leadership. As transformational leaders, they inspire those around them to make changes based on the shared mission and goals of the school. As distributed leaders, they empower multiple leaders within the school to share decisionmaking power, build trust and ownership, and incorporate feedback from multiple sources (Spillane, Halverson, & Diamond, 2001). As instructional leaders, decisions are aligned to support teaching and learning in the instructional core (Hallinger, 2005). Leadership is often shared among principals, assistant principals, teachers, counselors, and other staff, who work collectively toward the same end.

These schools' principals are also hands-on instructional leaders, well-versed in curriculum, instruction, and formative assessment practices, and not afraid of working with students, teachers, families, and community partners in improving instruction at every level (Cuban, 1984; Hallinger, 2003). This ensures that decisions affecting the school, such as master schedules and academic requirements, are aligned to the teaching and learning that takes place inside classrooms.

In addition to being multifaceted leaders, these school principals balance courage and strategy in enacting tough decisions, and work tirelessly to recruit and retain staff that share and act on the school's vision for its students. Finally, these leaders are entrepreneurial and cultivate numerous beneficial relationships with partners and stakeholders to advance the missions of their schools.

Within this design element of leadership, its essential components include:

- **Setting Clear and Achievable Goals.** Leaders motivate, define, and refine specific, measurable, process- and outcomes-focused goals that attend to students' knowledge and language development.
- **Demonstrating Deep Knowledge about Literacy and Language Development.** Leaders foster shared beliefs and deepened understanding of students' language and cultural strengths, and inherent language development opportunities in content-area courses for the diversity of ELs—newcomers, SIFE, and biliterate, bilingual, or multilingual learners.
- **Supporting Opportunities for Teachers to Learn and Grow.** Leaders at the school ensure that teachers have the materials, resources, and professional learning opportunities that meet the changing needs of the student population within a culture of continuous improvement and reflection.

This chapter focuses on leadership examples from three schools that had numerous individuals spearheading efforts to enable students to excel in college and careers. Although each school approaches leadership in distinct ways—from shared leadership to a stance of social justice—the leaders, teachers, and staff all work seamlessly as a team to support EL success.

IT TAKES A VILLAGE ACADEMY

Principal Marina Vinitskaya and her assistant principals are key figures in It Takes A Village Academy's continued growth and student success. Vinitskaya took leadership in 2007 with a clear vision of the kind of school that she wanted to co-create. The vision that she had for ITAVA was that every student would be respected and would thrive academically. She said:

> We have a very heavy immigrant population . . . children who come from low-performing middle schools. If you don't respect what they bring, if you don't respect their parents, if you don't respect your colleagues . . . Yes, they might speak with an accent, but they have better knowledge [than you do] in the subject area.

An immigrant herself, she navigated the New York school system with her own children, and what she experienced frustrated her and gave her a fiery passion for enacting systemic change in the structures and supports for immigrant students. According to the 2015 School Quality Review Report, 97% of ITAVA teachers—as opposed to 85% citywide—report that the principal displays instructional leadership (New York City Department of Education, 2017).

Demonstrating Deep Knowledge about Literacy and Language Development

The members of the administration at ITAVA understand that leaders' actions can establish the vision and the pedagogical design of the school, and they show their staff their commitment by leading and supporting schoolwide and pedagogical efforts and changes that they believe will better meet students' needs. For example, Vinitskaya became certified to provide WestEd's Quality Teaching for English Learners (QTEL) professional development. She has encouraged school staff to take QTEL courses as well, and most of the teachers and administrators have done so.

Because Vinitskaya is strong in math and science, she hired an assistant principal who is strong in the liberal arts so that they would complement each other in providing supervision and leadership to teachers in the content areas. As a district leader explained:

> [Vinitskaya] understood right from the beginning that it's a school and you're the educational leader as the principal, and has stayed true to that. As much as she's good on the other end with the data and use of resources and the budget, she understands the eye on the prize is about the instruction.

Vinitskaya also demonstrates this commitment to instruction by personally tutoring students in math during the first period of the school day.

Supporting Opportunities for Teachers to Learn and Grow

ITAVA offers teachers numerous leadership opportunities and finds ways to provide them with the extra pay to support those roles. For example, both academic leaders and department leaders, chosen by seniority and expertise, are compensated. In addition, teachers are paid to teach in the before- and after-school tutoring programs. If teachers have a skill or interest, such as sports, robotics, or technology, they are encouraged to apply for funds to run a club or sports team. One teacher stated, "Everyone is involved in something." Teachers participate in hiring as well. Every year, teachers create a hiring committee that develops interviewing questions and takes part in vetting final candidates. Teachers also help observe lessons that are modeled by prospective candidates.

In addition, school leadership is entrepreneurial in applying for and obtaining grants for academic and extracurricular offerings at the school and in funding team teaching, extended learning programs, and extracurricular offerings. In describing some funding strategies, the principal explained the use of resources:

> Some teachers come at 8:30 a.m., some come at 9:30 a.m. I stagger their schedules. And then, I don't use money for too many administrative people on board. I, just now in our eighth year, hired a second VP, because our college and social-emotional component is a big one and we need someone to have those skills to oversee the program. I don't believe that [having] many assistant principals will make the difference. I believe that it's the quality of the people that make the difference.

The school leadership's inspirational commitment, deep involvement at all levels, unflagging focus on continuous improvement, and creative use of resources help explain why this school consistently provides such extraordinary outcomes.

MANHATTAN BRIDGES HIGH SCHOOL

A teacher at Manhattan Bridges describes her colleagues in the following way:

> We are a team of teachers that are not afraid of work. We understand that we might do double or triple the amount of work [that] some other schools [do], and we're not afraid of that. We're very daring, and if something needs to get done, we'll do our very best. [Principal Sanchez-Medina] has a very strong vision for the school, and that has kept us grounded. We know what we want. We know where we're going.

Behind the high-quality classroom instruction at Manhattan Bridges is an incredibly dedicated and experienced team of educators working together to serve its students, guided by a clear vision of the school's purpose.

Principal Sanchez-Medina, a migrant from Puerto Rico, a former EL, and a former bilingual high school science teacher, is intimately familiar with the life experiences of the students at her school, as well as with the demands that face a classroom teacher working with newcomer ELs. Since opening Manhattan Bridges High School, Sanchez-Medina has steadily built the school into a recognized college preparatory program for some of the city's most underserved students, while remaining extremely reflective about the work that still needs to be done.

A major strength of the leaders at the school is their keen understanding that building a successful school requires a forward-looking vision and a long process of continuous reflection and improvement. Guided by their vision of a high-performing school for Spanish-speaking newcomers, they have built a staff of people who share a common understanding of the school's mission, and they have gradually added layers and structures to the school. Principal Sanchez-Medina, for example, emphasizes that it takes a long time to create a successful school, and that the process requires a great deal of humility and hard work, as she explains:

> Don't look at the school where it is now. Look at the school where you want it to go, so that you are building your infrastructure, the staff, the professional development . . . that the common vision is built toward that. Every year, you are building a layer to get there. There has to be an understanding of where I want to go. And then there has to be a process of constructing. It doesn't just happen . . . you have to build that process. As you are building the structures, you need to build the people, the team, and you need to know them. There has to be a common understanding.

Being an effective leader also means being a learning leader. As Sanchez-Medina put it, "As a leader, you also need to [participate in professional development]. You need to check your ego at the door, and you need to sit down and learn. You need to assess your learning, where you are in this process." When she realized that she did not have sufficient knowledge of balanced literacy practices, for example, she attended professional learning workshops alongside her teachers so that she could learn for herself.

Although Manhattan Bridges has been recognized repeatedly for its many achievements, the school leaders readily acknowledge that they are still miles away from where they want to be, even if they are moving in the right direction. Sanchez-Medina celebrates the successes of her staff and students, reflected in a recent strong School Quality Review Report (New York City Department of Education, 2017), but she does not dwell on them. Rather, she focuses on the work that still needs to be done. Some of the school's future plans include a Grade 9–14 program that awards not just a high school diploma but also an associate degree; the introduction of the International Baccalaureate program; and the possible addition of a gifted program for ELs.

NEW WORLD HIGH SCHOOL

Steering the success of New World High School is a three-person leadership team, a group of energetic and passionate individuals who are highly invested in ensuring that all students receive a rigorous academic experience while obtaining English language proficiency. The three administrators—Principal Fausto Salazar and Assistant Principals Mithat Gashi and Hassan Tmimi, who immigrated from Ecuador, Albania, and Morocco, respectively—frequently draw on their own experiences as learners of English to design a program that specifically meets the needs of its diverse student body. As one example, the principal, describing the social-emotional services at the school, said, "I go back to my own experience as an immigrant. I was considered a middle-class student at home, but [in school here] I was at the bottom. You think that you'll never get out . . . so one of the things that we have is a very strong counseling team."

Staff who work with the leadership team describe them as close-knit, "finishing each other's sentences," and aligned with a common vision for the school. Principal Salazar worked closely with his team to build New World from the ground up. The visionary, strategic, and instructional leadership team has played an undeniably important role in the positive outcomes at New World High School by setting the tone for the entire school and by developing the necessary structures, programs, and instruction to ensure ELs' college and career readiness.

Setting Clear and Achievable Goals

Although an inspirational and visionary leadership team may help inspire and motivate the staff to work toward a shared vision, having a clear-cut strategy for how to achieve these goals is also necessary. At New World, the strategy for accomplishing goals for student outcomes emanates from the school's mission. A Fordham Network administrator explained that "[The school] focus is on learning English . . . and their methodology has grown out of this shared mission." The structure of the school is built on a pillar of student and teacher supports to ensure that nobody slips through the cracks.

Case study research has suggested that isolated interventions not aligned with the core mission of a school are less likely to result in desired student outcomes than are actions closely related to the objectives of the school (Datnow, Lasky, Stringfield, & Teddlie, 2006). At New World, the leadership is acutely aware that high levels of programmatic coherence are necessary to achieve schoolwide goals. Decisions spanning scheduling and external resources, for example, are always guided by the mission of the school. When asked about the most important elements for creating a successful program, Principal Salazar advised others to "look at the mission of the school . . . and do not deviate from it." He gave an example of a time when he was approached by an organization during his early years as a school principal at New World, and he had to make a difficult choice:

> An organization came and said, "We are going to give you this, this, and this. College trips, and tutoring classes." You name it . . . I said, "Okay. What do you need from us?" And they said, "I need you to separate the kids. I want the kids that are going to the fields of medicine . . ." And I said, "What are you really asking for here?" Basically, they wanted the 'best' kids. And I said, "I can't do that . . . I think these kids are going to do well wherever they go, but I need resources for the other kids . . . I want what you are offering for *every* kid. I cannot go back and tell some kids that you can have this but others can't." That's not what this school is about.

As careful decisionmakers, the leadership team ensures that the activities that take place at New World are aligned with the core mission of the school. The assistant principals, for example, described their programmatic approach toward "early success." The school schedule gives students extra instructional time to ensure that students become high achievers early in their academic career. Ninth- and 10th-graders take two periods each of integrated math and English each day to get up to speed. Students are continually assessed and moved out to more advanced work when ready. Principal Salazar noted that this strategy allows the school to save resources for the later years, since the intensive support in 9th and 10th grade helps to prepare students for more advanced courses, reducing the need for remedial help as students progress.

Beyond conserving resources, this strategy also helps the school target academic interventions in more productive ways. Because ELs face particular challenges in becoming college- and career-ready, such as overcoming language barriers while being held to the same rigorous standards of learning as English Proficient students, time is a valuable resource. Studies have shown that it can take ELs four to seven years to achieve academic English proficiency (Hakuta, Butler, & Witt, 2000), so intensive interventions and increased instructional time early in their high school careers are critical to ensuring that they graduate on time and ready for college and careers.

Demonstrating Deep Knowledge about Literacy and Language Development

Research indicates that as instructional leaders of the school, administrators must be knowledgeable about instructional issues and focused on aligning programs and structures at the school to improve instructional practices (Elmore, 2000). The leadership team at New World ensures that they are involved in all matters of instruction. They understand the language and literacy practices required by the new standards and the inclusion of ELs in new standards-aligned instruction (Valdés et al., 2014). The group helped develop the curriculum and instructional structure for the school from its inception, attending to language and literacy development within the content areas, and frequently they conduct observations and provide instructional feedback to their staff. An external provider explained:

> I've been in many, many schools, and this is one of the few schools I've been to where the principal goes to observe classrooms. There are a lot of principals who do not do that and simply delegate the task to the assistant principals . . . I join them, and we all go in together to see science classes. . . . After the observation, we will spend about half an hour to an hour discussing the ratings and the justification for the ratings.

The leadership team's expertise plays a large role in their ability to do this. Collectively, the three administrators at New World taught math and social studies for over 25 years at the secondary level, and Assistant Principal Gashi at the postsecondary level as well. All three leaders have worked with ELs throughout their careers across the communities they have served. An instructional consultant explained, "They *were* teachers, and they have gone through so many different systems. . . . You respect a person who has been in the classroom. They have taught, and they know how to talk to staff."

Supporting Opportunities for Teachers to Learn and Grow

Research on school leadership is prolific, and there are endless debates about what constitutes an effective leadership style for a principal. However, some researchers note that transformational leaders are highly effective in stimulating and empowering followers to achieve extraordinary outcomes (Bass & Riggio, 2006)—these leaders are accessible, supportive of staff, and communicative.

At New World, the entire leadership team exhibits these traits common to inspirational and visionary leaders. Faculty and staff frequently described them as collaborative, cooperative, responsive, strongly attentive to the needs of each individual student, and united around a common vision for the school. According to Assistant Principal Gashi, he and the other administrators frequently engage in "ongoing formal and informal dialogue with teachers on topics that improve the school environment, student learning, and teacher professional growth."

One community partner mentioned that they had never seen a team work together with such collaboration. As an example of the unity between the administrators, an external provider recounted his experience working with the team on a professional development activity:

> It was not required . . . but, as a group, the three of them observed each teacher together. They *insisted* upon doing every single one of the observations together. What does this represent? First of all, this represents a holistic picture of the staff . . . . They are aligning their own practices around assessment so that there is interrater reliability . . . I have never seen a leadership team spend as much time talking, aligning, reaching consensus. And then, of course, the entire faculty picks up on this.

The principal and assistant principals were also described as placing a personalized focus on each student at the school. According to one external provider, "They don't try to fit a square peg into a round hole. They look at each student individually." Support staff indicated that the leadership team members, in addition to regularly meeting with counselors and other staff to obtain an update about the progress of students, also make themselves accessible to students. One teacher explained, "When I tell other people that the assistant principals help students, they can't believe it. [The assistant principals] will sit down with [students], and they will go over work with them."

The entire teaching team also shared how they felt inspired, valued, and respected by the leadership team. One staff member indicated, "I don't feel like I'm coming to work every day. It's a joy. This is my family." Another teacher mentioned that the principal is always communicating with the school staff to ask, "What do you think about this idea?" A previous teacher at the school also noted how New World's leaders inspired her to improve as an educator:

> Mr. Tmimi made me a better administrator. That was hard for me because it didn't come naturally, but I enjoyed my role as the administrative head of [a] department. I wanted to prove to Tmimi that I could do it. I wanted to get better for him to see that I could do it. I honestly believe that the reason New World is successful is not because of individual student success or because each one of the teachers are necessarily amazing (although that's probably true too!). A big part of New World's success is . . . [that] the culture of the school motivates teachers to do better than just "good enough." The leadership and culture of the school holds teachers accountable and motivates teachers to expect more of themselves . . . [My previous] experience [has] taught me how rare and special it is to work for an organization that has strong leaders.

Beyond being highly collaborative, respectful, communicative, and in-spiring, the leadership team also puts forth a clear vision for New World High School that focuses on providing support structures for ELs and teach-ers. The assistant principals explained that all staff and faculty must be familiar with what they are doing and how they are doing it with relation to the larger school vision—it is something everyone needs to believe in and know at the school. An external provider observed, "The teachers see the same vision, working toward high performance. They see the vision that the leadership sees. So it's really a team collaboration." A staff member agreed, noting, "There is a lot of collaboration among us all to figure out how to service the students."

CONCLUSION

The leaders of all of the schools in this study embody the fourth design element of successful high schools for ELs. All can be described as passion-ate, strategic, and driven by their mission to help all ELs succeed. They are courageous in their decisionmaking, tireless in their efforts to recruit and retain staff whose vision and teaching practices align closely with their own, and masterful in the cultivation of relationships that serve to advance the mission of the school. Three components were found to be essential to their strong and successful leadership: (1) setting clear and achievable goals, (2) demonstrating deep knowledge about literacy and language development, and (3) supporting opportunities for teachers to learn and grow.

At New World High School, setting clear and achievable goals is tightly linked to enacting only those programs and interventions that align with the school's mission. The school's focus on learning English guides all decision-making at the school, whether it is related to budgets or class schedules. It is absolutely understood by the school's leadership that high levels of pro-grammatic coherence are essential to achieving schoolwide goals. Research has shown, in fact, that isolated interventions not aligned with the core mission of a school are less likely to result in desired student outcomes than are actions closely related to the objectives of the school (Datnow et al., 2006). Taking the time to develop deep knowledge about the acquisition of language and literacy also contributes to a school's success. During a school-wide effort to implement WestEd's Quality Teaching for English Learners (QTEL), the principal of It Takes a Village Academy became certified by WestEd to provide the training. She continued to provide this training for several years afterward. Clearly, one cannot lead without expertise in the field in which teachers are expected to excel. The third component of this design element, supporting opportunities for teachers to learn and grow, is exemplified by the leadership of New World High School, where, in addition to providing regular opportunities for professional learning, administrative leaders frequently engage in informal dialogue with teachers on topics that improve the school environment, student learning, and teacher professional growth.

The fifth design element of successful high schools for ELs—strategic staffing and teacher development—is discussed in the following chapter.

CHAPTER 5

Design Element 5
Strategic Staffing and Teacher Development

It's more about professional learning, not professional development where we're doing something to them. It's about learning together. (an instructional coach at Dual Language)

Following a focus in the previous chapter on the design element of school leadership, we next take up the companion design element of staffing and professional development. Schools are human resource-intensive, and the professional capacity of the faculty and staff is an essential feature of schools that advance student achievement (Bryk, Sebring, Allensworth, Easton, & Luppescu, 2010). Schools thrive largely as a result of their ability to recruit and retain high-quality faculty, support their professional development, and organize their ability to work together to improve instruction. Across these schools in our study, we observed elements of rigorous, intentional, and strategic hiring and staffing practices. These practices have produced teams of diverse, passionate, empathetic, and instructionally innovative teachers and support staff to drive success for ELs.

The educators who work in these schools have been assembled deliberately to meet the multifaceted needs of students. School staff members, including leaders, often are immigrants and former ELs, speak students' home languages, and have significant international travel experience. Schools work in collaboration with teacher preparation institutions in recruiting diverse teacher candidates who have the potential to succeed at their sites. Teachers are recruited for their diversity of language and cultural perspectives and experiences, and serve as role models for students. They are also often dual-certified in ESL and content areas. The combination of a staff's multicultural histories, along with its deep knowledge of working with ELs, helps teachers hone in on the strengths and needs of the EL populations at their site.

New staff members who share the school's vision and meet high standards are actively recruited. Across schools, the school community—including teachers and students—is highly involved in the vetting of candidates. This egalitarian approach to hiring ensures that new teachers are aligned to schools' values and committed to helping their students reach high academic expectations.

After going through a rigorous and intentional hiring process, teachers are then supported throughout the various stages of their career by an array of professional learning opportunities that address their needs and strengths. These individuals are charged to learn from their own practice and develop their professional teaching expertise among a community of peers (Darling-Hammond & Bransford, 2007). Teachers are in charge of their own professional learning, which is tailored to their particular needs and aligned to the mission of the school. Collaboration is frequent and structurally well-supported, and retention levels are high.

Within the design element of strategic staffing and teacher development, the essential components include:

- *Recruitment of Teachers with Strong Knowledge of Content and Language Development.* Teachers have the pedagogy and formative assessment practices that accelerate academic development for ELs and are likely multilingual.
- *Classroom and School Culture of Mutual Respect and Learning.* Teachers have deep knowledge of and experience with engaging and communicating with ELs.
- *Openness to Learn and Grow as a Part of a School Community.* Team members participate and lead in professional learning opportunities and are reflective and continuous lifelong learners.

As noted earlier, the five schools profiled in this chapter recruited and developed their school team in deliberate ways. Teachers, staff members, and school leaders we interviewed all have a depth of knowledge of the history, background, needs, and strengths of the ELs in their school communities. This distinct knowledge about the EL and/or immigrant experience deeply shapes the motivations and drive of the educators who have chosen to work within these learning communities. The staff and leadership's pride and respect for the diversity of students' cultures and languages are reflected in their work with students and families during this important phase of transition from adolescence into young adulthood.

BOSTON INTERNATIONAL HIGH SCHOOL AND NEWCOMERS ACADEMY

Staff, students, and family members alike at BINcA see the diversity of the student body as one of the school's most valuable strengths. One student explained that she likes her school because even though students come from different countries, they do not act differently with different groups; instead, they work as one group and help one another. Another student describes

BINcA as very diverse, but a place where everyone gets along with one another, people do not feel separated, and no one group feels like it is better than another. Families of students at BINcA also appreciate the many cultures, languages, countries, and religions represented by the school's students, and the ways in which teachers draw upon students' backgrounds when they are teaching. As one parent put it, since the United States is a multicultural country, a multicultural school like BINcA will help prepare students for college and life after high school.

Classroom and School Culture of Mutual Respect and Learning

BINcA hires diverse staff members who possess keen understanding of the immigrant experience and the language skills with which to communicate with students and their families. For example, staff members speak many of the home languages used by students, from Spanish to Cape Verdean Creole, Haitian Creole, and Arabic. Family members feel more at ease, welcomed, and willing to become more involved when families and staff can communicate in shared languages. Beyond the connection of shared language, many staff members also draw from their personal experiences as immigrants or refugees to build connections with their students and their struggles. For example, the guidance counselor is empathetic toward her students because she is also an immigrant. Regarding the shared experiences that she and many staff members have with their students, she explained:

> Many of us are products of immigrant parents, so we easily connect, understand [our students] and their struggles. Maybe they don't have all of their family, or have access to resources and family helping them to navigate their new world because family members may be studying and working full-time. It takes one-on-one time where we build relationships and trust with each student, then you can build their self-esteem.

Staff members at BINcA also use their understandings of their students' various cultural customs and backgrounds as a resource when working with students and their families. The guidance counselor explained a recognition that school personnel have in working with immigrant families:

> When it comes to decisions about college, there are a number of reasons parents may not be directly involved. It could be because of work, or because of other family responsibilities, or the lack of time, or [because they are] embarrassed about their lack of education or language barriers. From my family's perspective, a student goes to school, [and] the teacher and [headmaster] are in charge of that student and there's no reason for parents to be involved—because they are taken care of.

The school team often takes on significant responsibility for helping families explore opportunities and recognize possibilities for their children. The ability of the BINcA team to speak the families' home languages puts many families at ease, but challenges persist. The guidance counselor recalls how families may encourage their children to work, rather than pursue college, because of the high cost of college. The team understands that there is a both a generational and cultural shift at play, and they see their role as supporting both the child's and family's long-term success in this new country.

Staff members at BINcA also use their knowledge of diverse cultures to ensure that students receive the supports they need. Recognizing that seeking counseling is viewed with a stigma in some cultures, staff members are careful to frame referrals to the counselor as "checking in at the health center" or "meeting with someone to see how you are liking the school." By changing the description of counseling to make it more acceptable to students, adults at BINcA deftly steer students toward the services they need to be successful.

That the staff members at BINcA are uniquely attuned to the needs of students because of the staff's diverse language and cultural backgrounds is not lost on family members, who are quick to note that the school hires for diversity of backgrounds, cultures, and languages. Parents and caregivers take comfort in the fact that school staff members who come from similar backgrounds as students and their families are more likely to be sensitive to their cultural heritages and educational needs. It is this deliberate attention to understanding and valuing the cultural background and assets of families that allows the school team to close the distance between culturally diverse families and the school culture (Valdés, 1996).

Openness to Learn and Grow as a Part of a School Community

During her years as the school's leader, former Headmaster Bahnam assembled a team that cares about and knows how to work with BINcA's diverse student population. In assessing the viability of potential teacher candidates, Bahnam discussed three major criteria she used in guiding her decision:

1. *Candidate's depth of knowledge in her or his content area*—Can this teacher work with students toward a high level of rigor?
2. *Candidate's experience and familiarity with teaching ELs and SIFE*—How does this teacher design his or her units and lessons for ELs and maintain student engagement in learning the content and developing language?
3. *Candidate's interactions with BINcA students*—How does this teacher respond to student questions and replies? What feedback do students have about this potential candidate?

The former headmaster was not afraid to be tough with her staff and hold people accountable. In her evaluation of teachers, she visited classrooms and described everything she saw and heard. Afterward, she asked herself what she learned and where she was lost. She also reflected on the deeper understandings that were engendered by the lesson, looking at the quality of the questions that the teacher asked the students, what types of scaffolds he or she may have used, and whether the lesson was thoughtfully planned and executed. In some cases, Bahnam had to dismiss teachers who were not a good match for the school's priorities and vision, and she viewed this as necessary to keep students at the center of her decisionmaking.

Going hand-in-hand with the commitment to success at BINcA is an openness to feedback that characterizes a growth mindset (Dweck, 2006). Neither the administrators nor the teachers are content with the progress the school has made. There is a willingness to talk about their perceived weaknesses, a sense that "we're not there yet." The staff at the school is motivated to keep refining its practices, such as starting an advisory system to better support students, and creating curriculum maps across grades and content areas to build a more coherent program of learning for students.

HIGH SCHOOL FOR DUAL LANGUAGE AND ASIAN STUDIES

What stands out about the instructional staff at Dual Language is their reflective nature, tremendous openness to sharing their practice, and motivation to collaborate and learn from one another. The dedicated, mission-driven staff at Dual Language was recruited and is supported by an administration led by the founding principal, Li Yan, and Assistant Principal Miriam Uzzan. In building their school team, Principal Yan and Assistant Principal Uzzan recruit educators with strong content knowledge and deep experiences working with ELs. Candidate teachers are hired based on the needs of the school community, as well as their strengths and potential for growth in a bilingual instructional setting and motivation and passion for working with the Dual Language student population.

While all the teachers here are experts in their own disciplines, they also have a mindset of continuous improvement to maximize the academic aspirations and potential for their students. Everyone takes responsibility and works as a team to make sure every student leaves Dual Language biliterate in English and Chinese, and ready to be successful in postsecondary institutions.

New teaching staff, who have made it past two rounds of sample lessons and multiple interviews with the principal and assistant principal, are matched up with a formal mentor or colleague who can help them adapt to a new school culture and provide necessary guidance and resources to be successful with the students. These mentor/mentee relationships are fluid. In addition to having formal mentors, new teachers often organically gravitate toward colleagues who are in the same subject area or work with the same students. For example, the ESL teachers and content teachers collaborate informally during their Friday professional learning time. ESL teachers talked about working with the content-area teachers in their grades and trying to build on the themes and topics that students are learning in their core classes.

There is also a significant amount of informal learning among colleagues during their prep periods, before school, and after school hours. Teachers who are interested in observing a colleague's classroom or working with fellow teachers can request to have coverage for their classes if their prep periods do not overlap with one another. This practice has numerous benefits for the teaching staff. First, new teachers learn how their colleagues support student learning. Second, teachers have a chance to see how their own students interact and learn outside of their own classroom setting. Lastly, this practice of opening up teachers' classrooms supports a school culture where colleagues are encouraged to learn from one another.

More formally, the school works with an instructional coach, compensated by state and district professional learning funds, who interacts with individual teachers and co-plans with the leadership team during Friday afternoon work sessions from 1:30–3 p.m. The instructional coach described her work:

> We look at data. We observe classrooms by visiting teachers. We survey the teachers and together do the [professional learning] calendar. It's organic. It's a needs-based development for teachers. We did decide that this year, we focus on "mindsets" and "knowing your students"—and we went from there.

The coach has collaborated on and off with the school team for the past decade, working closely with teachers in refining their practice, and helping teachers integrate new strategies into the teaching and learning culture in their classrooms. It is not about doing some "strategy of the week," by which teachers are forced to try out ideas without input on how they will improve learning. Instead, the coach works with the teachers and encourages them to lead their own classroom inquiry by asking reflective questions about their own teaching, gathering student feedback and data on what's working, and trying out approaches that improve student learning.

MANHATTAN BRIDGES HIGH SCHOOL

The "beautiful thing" about Manhattan Bridges, according to one teacher we spoke to, is that it is staffed by people who care about what they do and who are willing to put in the extra time. He described the faculty as a "learning community" made up of teachers who have a passion for teaching and learning. The teachers trust that there is a solid vision in place and a team of hardworking people willing to put it into action. The teachers are also very flexible in responding to the needs of the school. One science teacher with a background in biology taught herself how to do computer coding so that she could teach the technology course on campus. The staff is comprised of experienced, veteran teachers, many of whom have worked with ELs for a long time.

That Manhattan Bridges is staffed by a team of highly driven, dedicated, and experienced teachers is far from accidental. Bringing onboard a talented group of educators has been an intentional part of the school-building process, and the school's hiring and coaching practices reflect this emphasis on teacher quality as a priority.

In her hiring process, Principal Sanchez-Medina first assesses the needs of the school in terms of programming. She figures out what subject area, field of expertise, or group of students requires additional staffing. Next, she thinks about how a new hire would potentially fit into the existing team—perhaps she needs someone to lead an initiative on campus, or a team player who will get along well with other subject-area or grade-level teachers. Once she has weighed the needs of her program along with the needs of her team, she develops a very specific profile of the kind of staff member she needs to hire. And once she has developed this profile, she does not settle—she waits for the right person to fill the role.

In addition to assessing a candidate's fit with the needs of her program and the team, Principal Sanchez-Medina also looks for mature professionals who can model proper behavior and ethics to their students. Because of the student population at Manhattan Bridges, Principal Sanchez-Medina also requires that her teachers be willing to attain a bilingual extension or ESL certification for their teaching credential. Another set of qualities she looks for are those of a caretaker—someone who can see all children's potential. To this end, she looks for candidates who understand child and adolescent development and care deeply about guiding students to maximize their potential.

After screening prospective candidates with an initial interview, Principal Sanchez-Medina invites the selected candidates to campus to meet with a panel of interviewers composed of teachers, staff members, family members, and sometimes students. The interview panel asks questions of the candidates related to classroom management, instruction, planning, student voice, and involvement with the community and with extracurricular activities. The panel also asks candidates about their strengths and areas of growth. Finally, candidates teach a demo lesson to showcase their instruction. If the interview panel advocates for a candidate moving forward in the interview process, the candidate is invited back to meet and attend meetings with the team he or she will be working with, so that the team members can make sure the candidate is a good match for them.

Once a candidate successfully passes through the rigorous hiring process, the new staff member is paired with at least one mentor within the same discipline to help ensure a smooth transition to the school. Principal Sanchez-Medina holds the new teachers to high expectations, yet she provides them with ample support and coaching. Assistant Principal Lock shared, "We aim to hire people with strong content knowledge, and then we develop their pedagogical expertise." For Principal Sanchez-Medina and other administrators on campus, supervision of their teachers is not just an evaluative process. Rather, it is an ongoing dialogue with teachers that involves pre-work, coaching, modeling, and reflection to promote their development. One teacher described the coaching and mentoring relationship in the following manner:

> I have worked closely with [Assistant Principal] Lock, since the beginning of 2012. Throughout our 3-year work relationship . . . he has not only demonstrated to be a very competent supervisor, but also a mentor and coach. Most important, he properly supports the development of teachers. Through his coaching style of supervision, he allows teachers such as myself to constantly improve upon their practice by soliciting self-reflection and actionable goals. His nonjudgmental inquiry approach greatly enhances a teacher's ability to plan, reflect, and problem-solve in ways to bring about high student achievement. For example, though many teachers at the school are rated "effective" and "highly effective," we are encouraged to share best-teaching practices and resources, and form inquiry teams to further improve pedagogy.

Imparting the same growth mindset that characterizes the principal's leadership of the school, administrators encourage teachers to reflect constantly about what is working in their classrooms, what can be improved, and what their commitments are for the following year. If teachers hit a rut, administrators work with teachers to find a solution.

Principal Sanchez-Medina sees her role as one of encouraging people to enable them to make a difference and transform. When she and other administrators see examples of excellent instructional practices, they celebrate these successes by highlighting them in staff emails or at faculty meetings. On the other hand, if teachers are not willing to grow in their practice, Sanchez-Medina is also not hesitant to suggest that they might not be a good fit for the school.

As a result of the deliberate and careful teacher selection process and the attention to teachers' ongoing professional learning and growth, the turnover at Manhattan Bridges has been relatively low. During the 2012–13 academic year, for example, the turnover rate stood at 11%, and 66% of the teaching staff had a master's or doctoral degree. Overall, the teaching staff is experienced, with most of teachers having spent more than ten years teaching at the school—and approximately half of the teachers have been at the school for their entire teaching careers. At the time of this study, the school has 28 teachers who are fully bilingual in Spanish and English, and almost all have bilingual extension credentials. Finally, teachers come with diverse backgrounds in engineering, politics, computer science, and literature.

MARBLE HILL HIGH SCHOOL

To carry out the vision and mission of Marble Hill, the leaders of the school have put together an experienced team of educators. Although not quite as diverse as the student body they serve, the teaching staff at Marble Hill consists of individuals who have lived outside of the country, who speak other languages, and who place value on language and diversity. Most teachers are ESL-certified, have travel experiences, and speak another language. They were in the U.S. Peace Corps or the Japan Exchange Teaching (JET) Program, like to travel, and have lived abroad. Most important, the school has experienced staff members who know the mission of the school. There is very little teacher turnover.

Recruitment of Teachers with Strong Knowledge of Content and Language Development

The assembling of this team requires that Marble Hill staff actively recruit and seek out candidates who have strong knowledge of content and language development and "fit" with the culture of the school. All teachers are carefully chosen through a deliberate hiring process. First, prospective teachers are interviewed by both school administrators and other teachers. Next, they are asked to conduct a demo lesson for all kinds of students (including general education, EL, and special education). After the demo lesson, the observing administrators, teachers, and students provide feedback. Teacher candidates may give their own assessment about the lesson regarding what went well and what did not go so well, including how their instructional practices impacted the diverse learners in the classroom. Sometimes there is a "mock process" to determine how well aspiring applicants work with others at the school. For example, the school examines the dynamics of group planning sessions as the applicant interacts with other teachers from the school. Overall openness to feedback is a key characteristic they consider when making hiring decisions. They only hire people who are open to feedback and understand how to support diverse learners.

Openness to Learn and Grow as a Part of a School Community

Marble Hill teachers meet by grade level and subject matter to problem-solve, design lessons, and share strategies to address students' needs. Professional learning at the school is strategic and regular, and teacher collaboration is abundant, both structured and unstructured.

The New York City Department of Education mandates four professional learning days per academic year. At Marble Hill, however, professional learning is planned weekly, and Wednesdays are shortened days for students to allow teachers a common time. During these hours, the staff receives training on a variety of instructional approaches. For example, teachers have learned to use the Danielson (2011) framework, a tool that helps educators identify elements of teaching that promote student learning. The school has a committee to help make decisions about the professional learning opportunities. One person from each discipline is represented, and the group sets the professional learning agenda for the year.

Teachers also use their professional learning time to focus on a specific issue or "inquiry." A schoolwide practice since 2002, the goal of a teacher inquiry is to develop a set of strategies and interventions that work for a broader group of students by testing interventions on a smaller group of students. Teams of teachers, typically organized by grade level, study the academic performance of a set of focal students. In their classrooms, the teachers then implement a variety of strategies to test and uncover approaches that help to increase their students' academic and language development.

All teachers at the school are part of two teams, disciplinary and grade-level groups, that work on curricular development, grade-level articulation, and general support for one another. These grade-level and departmental groups also work in collaboration with ESL teachers to co-plan units. For example, 11th- and 12th-grade teams work together to develop a coherent scope of sequence in courses such as U.S. Literature, and collaborate with ESL counterparts in incorporating language and literacy development supports for ELs in those classes. Although certain types of collaborations are structured, there are also a lot of informal opportunities for co-planning. One teacher observed, "There is a lot of informal collaboration in the break room," and another noted, "Teachers share with others as learning partners." Another staff member said:

> There is so much informal collaboration at this school. Any time you go into the staff room, you get that . . . Like the two [Global Studies] teachers are going to be working together to make sure that they are moving at the same pace. The math teachers are doing the same thing. Right now the Algebra ESL is a unit behind so they are all trying to figure out how to pick that up.

The culture of collaboration makes it possible for teachers to design interdisciplinary, project-based learning lessons that are stimulating and engaging for students. Beyond this, collaboration also encourages teachers at Marble Hill to learn from one another as part of an ongoing process of developing and honing their instruction to better meet the needs of their students.

NEW WORLD HIGH SCHOOL

The New World staff is culturally and linguistically diverse. Administrators themselves speak four different languages—Spanish, Arabic, Albanian, and French—and the school hires teachers and staff who are sensitive to the needs of ELs. The staff's shared cultural experiences with students help them to serve more easily as role models for students. New World recruits its multicultural workforce through collaborations with local colleges, generating a pipeline that has attracted committed teachers to the school. Currently, five staff members at the school completed an internship at the site. The staff carefully reviews applications and résumés of prospective employees. Assistant Principal Mithat Gashi shared that they "take [their] time to thoroughly discuss challenges, expectations, and supports with prospective staff who apply for a position." The result is a young, multiethnic, multicultural staff that is highly committed to the vision of the school.

Since 2008, all teachers at New World receive training on conducting action research. The school was interested in developing an action research program to formalize its vision and procedures. Initially, New World invited consultants from Lehman College to help their staff learn how to develop questions and brainstorm issues to research. The first year, a Lehman College faculty member provided targeted training for teachers to conduct classroom action research. Since then, Assistant Principals Gashi and Tmimi have met with individual teachers to provide guidance, support, and training on classroom action research on a yearly basis. Principal Salazar related that there is a protocol that teachers must follow, but that they can decide on "basically any area" in which to conduct their research, including pedagogy, homework and its effects on outcomes, or use of technology.

Aligned with the core values of the school, this form of professional learning is intended to promote *ongoing* critical examination of instruction among teachers. They are expected to test their own hypotheses of instructional practices and adjust the delivery of instruction based on the results of their inquiry. Most important for teachers of ELs, this inquiry involves not just teaching and learning but the social and environmental elements of the classroom that may impact outcomes for students. In this sense, the process is an opportunity for teachers to learn about how students learn language and content as well as how students experience the classroom environment.

The principal indicated that action research is a way to "minimize misconceptions and look at actual data." For example, if there is an impression that students do not want to participate in challenging material, this may just be "an idea circulating among staff" that is not based on data. In an effort to diminish these types of misconceptions, action research actively aims to remove some of the guesswork. Teachers commonly use this work to implement changes in their practice. One action research inquiry led to the realization that teachers needed to reduce the volume of homework to prevent students from being overwhelmed. However, the principal noted, "You don't compromise rigor. You make adjustments."

Within the ongoing framework of action research, faculty meets with administrators every year to review student writing and data on assessments. Together, the administrators and teachers go over how to set goals for the year, establish research questions, and reflect on student work. Since teachers loop with, or follow, the same group of students every year, it is possible for teachers and administrators to set specific goals for each student. As the year goes on, teachers take notes on their research question, analyze student data, and share their findings with fellow teachers and administrators. Based upon these findings, they make changes to their teaching or shift the way they deliver instruction and reflect further on the changes made. The process involves observing and supporting student and teacher growth. Administrators provide feedback to facilitate this process using rubrics and in-person meetings, and participating teachers make a formal presentation to the school team at the end of the year. All results from the action research activities are posted on a shared drive accessible to the entire staff and faculty for future use.

CONCLUSION

The fifth design element of successful high schools for ELs consists of strategic staffing and teacher development. Essential components include: (1) the recruitment of teachers with strong knowledge of content and language, (2) a classroom and culture of mutual respect and learning, and (3) an openness to learn and grow as part of the school community.

Manhattan Bridges exemplifies the practice of recruiting teachers who are strong in both content and language. Their process for determining the characteristics of the right match for the school is extremely rigorous. Taking into account the needs of the program and the needs of the school, the principal develops a specific profile of the type of individual to be hired. The principal is also careful to find teachers who possess or are willing to earn bilingual or ESL certification. After participating in an interview with a panel of diverse stakeholders, the candidate is asked to teach a lesson. If, after all of these steps, the candidate is still in the running, he or she meets with potential team members to see if the fit is right.

The second component—cultivating a classroom and culture of mutual respect and learning—is exemplified by BINcA, which hires a diverse staff who possess a deep understanding of the immigrant experience and the language skills with which to communicate with students and their families. Family members feel more at ease, welcomed, and willing to become more involved when families and staff can communicate in shared languages.

Exemplifying an openness to learn and grow as part of the school community, teachers at New World High School receive ongoing support on how to conduct action research projects and are encouraged to develop action research projects that match their own professional interests. At year's end, all results are shared with the entire school staff.

The next chapter delves into the sixth design element of successful high schools for ELs—carefully orchestrated school structures.

CHAPTER 6

Design Element 6
Carefully Orchestrated Structures

> A belief in the power of schooling and our ability to improve this institution must also coexist with a modicum of doubt—a critical perspective—about the wisdom of any particular reform effort. Virtually every initiative involves at least some zone of wishful thinking, and even good designs typically require executing a strategy for which there is no established game plan.
> (Bryk, 2010, p. 30)

Foundational to a school's successful implementation of the design elements explored in the previous chapters is the creation of an organizational structure that supports ELs' progress toward graduating college- and career-ready. These schoolwide structures must be dynamic and flexible, and often are not bound by the regular class period or school day.

The most prevalent and impactful characteristic of the schoolwide structures of schools we studied is flexibility in their master schedules to accommodate students' various needs and push their learning to the fullest. One feature that distinguishes these schools' master schedules is the responsiveness of the school administration to adjusting students' schedules based on the most current information about their needs, despite the additional work this often entails. At some schools, students are given informal assessments each semester to gather up-to-date knowledge about their progress in language and content development. If a student's performance no longer matches the course placement, the school works quickly to adjust the student's schedule. The master schedule has been set up such that it is easy to make quick adjustments. The result is that students are not tracked into stock schedules by groups, but have highly individualized programs based on a combination of their language and subject-area needs.

The schools also take advantage of block scheduling and double-blocking certain courses to provide sufficient instructional time where it matters most, such as a double block of English and ESL to give students time to develop their language proficiency and literacy skills. Block scheduling allows teachers more instructional time per student and smaller roster sizes, and gives students more time on task and more time to practice critical thinking (Canady & Rettig, 1995; Thayer & Shortt, 1999).

Beyond careful attention to scheduling, the schools in our study recognize that the school day does not provide enough time to help students meet their rigorous academic demands. These schools extend the learning time through a combination of after-school tutoring, Saturday school, and summer programs. The availability of these additional learning opportunities ensures that students can always receive academic support when they need it.

In addition to creating thoughtful structures for students, these schools have also built structures that enable teachers to work with and learn from one another. Through early-release days or shared prep periods, teachers meet in grade-level teams to create interventions for struggling students, or in department teams to plan instruction, examine student work, and carry out data inquiry. The effort to make common planning time a priority at these schools allows teachers to deepen their practice and accelerate their professional learning.

Within this design element of carefully orchestrated structures, the essential components include:

- **Resources Organized to Create a Supportive Learning Environment.**
  A master schedule and flexibility in course options accommodate students' strengths and needs and are aligned to the school's language development framework and mission.
- **Extended Learning Time.** Student learning opportunities are created in and outside of the classroom, beyond the traditional school day and academic calendar year.
- **Targeted Learning Environments for Diverse Students.** Schools and classes are designed with students' prior experiences and interests at the forefront. This includes support and services to meet the needs of Recently Arrived English Learners (RAELs), commonly known as newcomers, and Students with Interrupted Formal Education (SIFE). Learning opportunities leverage student interests that support college and career readiness.

This chapter describes ways the six schools we studied organize their time, resources, and personnel so that all ELs receive the full support they need to graduate college- and career-ready and, in some cases, biliterate. There is not a single approach that is most effective. Each school starts with the students' needs and builds the appropriate infrastructure to meet the school's mission and vision for students and their families.

BOSTON INTERNATIONAL HIGH SCHOOL AND NEWCOMERS ACADEMY

BINcA optimizes students' engagement, learning, and effort through creative scheduling and rigorous coursework. Curriculum and graduation requirements include four years each of English, mathematics, and science, three years of history, two years of world languages, elective courses, and up to four years of ESL classes. Students must also complete a capstone independent research project in the 12th grade and have passing scores on state tests. Language and literacy development takes place not only in the double block of English, but is woven into the fabric of every single academic course at BINcA, as explained in Chapter 1. This practice gives students the foundation they need to be successful in postsecondary life after graduation.

Extended Learning Time

Former Headmaster Bahnam worked closely with her school community to provide BINcA's students with opportunities through a symbiotic balance between academic achievement and social-emotional supports. Bahnam recognized that the regular length of the school day is simply not enough time to prepare students to meet the rigorous academic demands of future college attendance and career performance. As a result, she worked tirelessly to procure additional funding that allows many teachers to work extended hours on Tuesdays and Thursdays from 2:45 p.m. to 4 p.m. Teachers tutor students in the 9th and 10th grades, as well as all newcomers. During Saturdays and semester breaks, teachers hold tutorials and offer intensive one-on-one and small-group help for students who need additional academic support.

It is an "all-hands-on-deck" type of environment at BINcA. Teachers and staff members are often seen working with students who are struggling with the coursework or challenged with how to express themselves through multiple literacies or feel understood in and out of the classrooms. With these academic support structures in place, students build confidence in their classes and feel prepared to take the Massachusetts Comprehensive Assessment System (MCAS) exams. One student expressed that with just an hour during the school day to learn math, she does not have time to learn everything. The after-school tutorial time allows her to extend her learning and solidify her understanding. The dean reported that BINcA has the highest attendance rate for Saturday school in the whole city, which is indicative of the students' desire to learn and improve. When the students know that there are so many adults backing them up, and that they are part of a community that will not let them slip through the cracks, they become fully committed to their academic success.

Targeted Learning Environments for Diverse Students

The Newcomers Academy, a distinct program within BINcA, came into existence as a result of an intentionally designed program to serve Boston's refugee student population and recent arrivals to the United States. These students spend one year receiving additional support in English and basic academic skills before entering the 9th or 10th grade, either at Boston International High School or another high school of their choice. If newcomer students are identified as Students with Interrupted Formal Education, they may spend up to two years in the Newcomers Academy building up literacy skills in both their native language and English before entering 9th grade. In the 2013–14 school year, 270 students designated as SIFE were enrolled in Boston Public Schools. About 20% of this SIFE population are enrolled in the Newcomers Academy at BINcA. Because it often takes SIFE longer than four years to graduate from high school, it is not atypical to find students between the ages of 18 and 22 in the upper grades at BINcA.

The following vignette provides a glimpse into the conversations that are taking place in one Native Language History class in the Newcomers Academy:

Six students, all of Haitian descent, are seated in a table cluster discussing why Haitians are immigrating to the United States and to other countries. The students speak animatedly and without reservation about the migration of Haitian people across the globe. Some share their thoughts on seeking better opportunities elsewhere. Others share their experiences of poverty, natural disasters, and corruption that have driven Haitians out of their own country.

In front of each student are population and topographical maps of Haiti and a handful of key phrases and vocabulary in both Haitian Creole and English. Their literacy/social studies teacher, Mr. G., who is of Haitian descent himself, moves the discussion toward uncovering root causes of this migration. He points to the maps and asks students to think about *who* those are who are fleeing the country, *how* they are transporting themselves, and *why*.

One student jumps in and talks about how girls in the Haitian countryside often do not have the same opportunities as boys to attend school. Meanwhile, others join in to talk about families who left and made better lives for themselves by any means possible. As the discussion heats up and moves intimately toward students' personal experiences, Mr. G. pulls the conversation back toward the larger thematic question posed for the unit: "What would your ideal country look like?"

Though the discussion is conducted mostly in Haitian Creole, Mr. G. occasionally introduces words in English to anchor the conversation and references some of the key phrases and vocabulary that strengthen and deepen students' means of expression in English.

The high level of agency and active participation seen in this vignette are typical in classes at the Newcomers Academy for SIFE. Students learn in small groups from teachers proficient in their native language, using a curriculum that is relevant, engaging, and adapted to students' needs.

The Newcomers Academy is a source of immense pride for the BINcA community. Former Headmaster Bahnam marveled at the progress of one Somali student who entered the Newcomers Academy last year. Even though Bahnam and the student shared Arabic as a common language, the student was hesitant to speak more than a couple of words. However, in her time at the Newcomers Academy, as Bahnam put it, "She got stronger, she got her foundation, she's ready, and now she's going to go places."

The progress that the SIFE population has made at the Newcomers Academy and Boston International High School is especially heartening. That 20% of the graduating class started as SIFE is what the headmaster considers the "real success" of BINcA. The close personal attention and extensive instructional supports that new arrivals and SIFE receive at the Newcomers Academy are an important reason for their success.

HIGH SCHOOL FOR DUAL LANGUAGE AND ASIAN STUDIES

The design of Dual Language is built upon explicit programming for the language development needs of its student body, with a conviction that all students will graduate with opportunities to attend and be successful in college. The leadership and staff have planned with care how school and classroom practices and structures work together to create a supportive and rigorous learning ecology for all their students, especially ELs and former ELs.

Resources Organized to Create a Supportive Learning Environment

The school structures its course sequences to maximize students' learning potential and avenues for growth, combining them with a strong teaching team that has expertise and facility in content and language development. For example, in addition to an expectation that all students achieve dual language fluency, all students take four years of mathematics and science courses. These courses include a range of AP courses available on campus taught by Dual Language staff as well as college credit-bearing courses that have been offered on-site by external faculty, and off-site course options made available to students. Flexibility is offered in the sequencing and development of mathematics courses, particularly with the topics covered in Algebra II and trigonometry courses. This set of math courses is designated as a college-readiness course that can be taken as a one- or two-year sequence. As a result, students have the option to move at a pace that best suits their needs and development in mathematics.

The assistant principal explains how the team conceptualizes the development and the structure of the learning pathways for students:

In both the Chinese and English departments, we look at where students are and how they are progressing in the language. It's hard to make every level one class the same, so we figure out what the students' strengths are and set the expectations. For EP students, we're trying to figure out their transition from English to Chinese. We ask ourselves, if students [native English speakers] were in China, what [would] they [be] expected to do? We're trying to make that curriculum more rigorous. . . . At the same time, we want the ESL students to improve their English, with the goal of a high pass on the ELA NY Regents.

Dual Language's underlying commitment to college-readiness requirements and biliteracy resonates through students' academic careers. This shared set of expectations guides the work of teachers, guidance staff, and the school leadership in their course planning based on student strengths and needs. This commitment to supporting students extends beyond the classroom and is further deepened by the school's robust guidance department. This team, composed of two full-time guidance counselors, a full-time family assistant, a full-time parent coordinator, and a half-time college counselor, meets weekly to set and revise goals, anticipate and tackle student-related needs, and organize programming that allows students to thrive academically, socially, and emotionally within and outside of the school community.

Throughout the year, the guidance and instructional teams work closely together to figure out how the ESL programming and course options can meet ELs' needs. For example, as students progress through the ESL levels, the course schedule needs to be flexible enough to support students who may be advancing more quickly or need additional supports. It is this collective effort and responsibility of the entire school community that works together in making its mission of college readiness and biliteracy a reality for its ELs.

In developing the course content and course sequences, the school team takes into consideration the strengths and needs of each incoming class as well as the growth and development of the current student body in both language and content knowledge development. That is, as appropriate, courses are designed to maximize students' learning time and preparation toward college and careers. This may mean creating a section for ESL-Biology class due to the interest and demand of 9th- and 10th-grade ELs interested in Biology, or an additional section of AP Calculus class to meet the growing interest and demand from the students. Each year, the instructional and counseling staff examines student data and creates courses that optimize students' language and academic development potential.

Courses are designed for college preparation, Regents exams, and enrollment in AP courses. Students take four years of English, social studies, math, and science, as well as four years of Chinese. Students in the 11th and

12th grades can take college-level courses in collaboration with New York University and as part of the City University of New York (CUNY) College Now Program offered by Baruch College, Hunter College, and the Borough of Manhattan Community College.

The school has prioritized language and literacy classes by blocking these classes into 90-minute daily periods, and some students may be taking multiple courses that focus on language and literacy if they are beginning ELs. Consequently, this prioritization of language and literacy instruction restricts the flexibility of courses for students, especially newcomers who have limited English proficiency. However, the school has wisely ensured that all ESL classes are credit-bearing, so students who are in ESL classes can accrue high school credit toward graduation. ESL and humanities teachers in the lower grades share a lot of collaboration and unit planning, as they work with the same students during the school day. At the same time, *all* students, both ESL and EP, take Chinese over the course of their academic careers and are prepared to take the AP Chinese exam in their junior or senior year. A writing center, run by New York University students, is open Monday through Thursday.

Extended Learning Time

Dual Language is also open on Saturday for college preparatory courses, physical education (PE), and supplementary workshops in English language development. College prep and SAT prep are offered through New York Cares on Saturday, when volunteers with this program work with students in small groups. The school has been able to take advantage of the campus facilities shared with four other schools and organize time on Saturday so students can complete their PE credit in an efficient manner. While our research team was not able to observe the learning activities that took place on Saturdays, the principal talked about what happens at the school on Saturdays from 9 am to 3:30 pm:

> We use Saturday school to do some instructional work. We have PE and additional ESL classes. Lots of kids want to be here. About 150 kids are here [on Saturdays]. They like to hang out, socializing, especially the EL kids. A lot of the kids live in the neighborhood. [During the weekdays], we allow them to stay until 6 p.m. They don't have space at home to do the work. Students will come to school on Saturday to do work.

Together with the intensive support provided by the counseling team, the school staff works together to ensure that students have opportunities that maximize learning time and prepare students for the rigors and demands of college.

Targeted Learning Environments for Diverse Students

Complementing Dual Language's deliberate approach to course sequencing and lesson design is the underlying deep passion and incredible drive that the school team has in supporting student success. Ms. B., an 11th-grade ELA and history teacher, attributed the school's success to "teachers' commitment and love for the student[s]." She said, "We work very hard and are dedicated to help[ing] everyone to improve. We work a lot of extra time, [doing] tutoring, support, and counseling." A former EL herself, Ms. B. shared her own history and experiences growing up, as she was forced to quickly assimilate and integrate into the dominant monolingual culture of schooling where she was in the United States. There, Ms. B. remembered her teachers explicitly telling her parents "*not* to speak Chinese . . . at home." Ms. B. was drawn to the mission of this school in developing "bilingual and bicultural citizens" who embody "curiosity and respect for American and Chinese cultures."

Similarly, Ms. C., a first-year ESL teacher at the school, wants her "students to have the language proficiency in English and Chinese to communicate effectively in both languages . . . [and] have both the language and thinking skills to advocate for themselves." This deep internal drive exemplified in both Ms. B. and Ms. C., paired with the teachers' openness to learning and improvement in their subject area and in language and literacy, encourages both students and teachers to be self-reflective and to learn from one another. When teachers are not facilitating student learning, they are reflecting on their own practice and learning from one another, formally in structured professional learning time as well as informally with colleagues with whom they share students. This highly motivated teaching staff also works closely to support the dynamic needs of the student population, and the school organizes itself for these demands and creates the appropriate learning opportunities to maximize student learning.

IT TAKES A VILLAGE ACADEMY

The dedicated, passionate teachers at It Takes A Village Academy are driven to impact the lives of their largely EL and immigrant student populations. Teachers have been able to maintain a high level of commitment because there are administrative structures that are in place to support high-quality teaching and learning experiences for their diverse student populations.

ITAVA offers their students a college-going program with rigorous, relevant, and varied curriculum, instruction, and assessment, and a staff committed to challenging and supporting their content and language development. The staff believes that with adequate support all students will master college preparatory coursework, and the school creates trajectories of opportunity that these students follow toward successful academic outcomes. In addition, much of this curriculum as well as numerous extracurricular offerings reflect the cultural backgrounds of the students. For example, soccer is a huge draw at this school because many of the students come from countries where it is the most popular sport.

ITAVA aligns resources, structures, and supports so that students can meet the high expectations set out for them, and the same creativity that is applied to the use of resources is seen in the planning of courses and schedules. For example, small classes, block scheduling, extended learning time, and advisories provide structural support to those ends. Fiscal resources are carefully allotted to provide programming and equipment that best meet the students' learning needs. The leadership team believes that traditional classroom schedules fail students and that course schedules need to be customized by the school to meet the needs of the population. Because of this, even the block schedule is not based on the most common forms of block scheduling wherein each class meets every other day for an extended period, but instead the leadership team makes deliberate and creative choices in scheduling to help individual students receive the lion's share of instruction in the areas that are most important for their academic success. For instance, students might meet for social studies six times a week, and animation class twice a week. In addition, the leadership strives to keep class sizes small so that ELs receive more individual attention. A typical English class size is 20 students, as compared to the citywide average of 25.8.

The leadership team programs each incoming student's day individually according to the student's needs in preparation for the Regents exams. It is the staff's absolute conviction that regardless of past educational experiences, ITAVA will prepare its students to achieve at high levels. The school understands that it is important for ELs to enroll in courses that will help them prepare for college-level academic work, and offers students a wide range of AP courses. The school finds that these opportunities are strong motivators and have a positive impact on students' perspectives on their own abilities. One teacher noted, "The Advanced Placement class I teach—that in itself is a motivation for my ELs. They feel elated, they are so honored that they are in that class." The leadership team believes that being an EL should not be a barrier to rigorous academic content. An achievement coach in the school network remarked, "[The students] may not have exact command of the English language, but [the teachers] put in place whatever is needed so that students can still achieve on grade-level content and beyond."

The school offers students seven weekly hours of English, with four hours focused on ELA and three focused on literature or culture. The teachers for these courses plan together so that their curriculum is aligned and affords teachers the opportunity to support students' content and skill development. In addition to four hours of math, students also take a two-hour History of Math course that is modeled after a course at New York City College of Technology. This course helps students understand where mathematical concepts came from, how they are applied in the world, and how they fit together, providing a purposeful learning experience. It also gives them a foundation in the discourse of mathematics so that they can successfully navigate the language demands of their practice-oriented math course. The teachers of the math and History of Math courses work together to align their curriculum so that students receive instruction in crucial concepts and information in concert with their regular math coursework. Moreover, ITAVA offers both regular grade-level science courses and a two-hour course in the literacy of the sciences. In addition to teaching discipline-specific academic language and literacy skills, this course supports scientific research skills.

Students take four hours of social studies, two hours of technology, and two hours of art classes per week. The leadership believes that arts education is extremely beneficial for ELs because it helps students acculturate to the U.S. context and allows students to share their own culture with their peers. This aligns with the Common Core's emphasis on the ability to understand other perspectives and cultures.

The school also offers separate language courses in Haitian Creole, French, Spanish, and Arabic so that students can continue to gain home language and literacy skills. These courses are either offered during the regular school day, or in Saturday school during extended programming. Students who are English Proficient can also choose among such language courses for their foreign language requirement.

MANHATTAN BRIDGES HIGH SCHOOL

The instructional design at Manhattan Bridges offers students the opportunity to take experiential STEM coursework that prepares them for postsecondary success. Students can choose between two STEM Academies—engineering or information technology (IT)—and they can apply to either the Transitional Bilingual Program (for newly arrived native Spanish speakers) or the Dual Language Spanish Program.

The school has partnerships with the National Academy Foundation to offer two career and technical education (CTE) academies for students, one in engineering and the other in information technology (IT) and computer science. Students who enter the school apply to one of the two academies. Students who successfully complete the IT program can receive industry certifications (e.g., in A+ and IC3) by the time they graduate, and students in the engineering academy have access to industry internships and credit-bearing college courses.

The power of these CTE academies is that they help students to see the immediate purpose of what they are learning in school for their future career aspirations. One student commented on her experience:

You have the opportunity to do [Work-Based-Learning] and job shadowing in and out of the academy. We have the opportunity to go to AT&T and NBC Universal to see the outside world. To see what it means to be in an office the entire day and to interact with professionals who are telling us about their experience and guide us. They review your résumé and give you networking skills. They help you with your personal development and expose you to what comes next.

In their pre-engineering or IT classes, students complete hands-on projects such as breaking down a computer or formatting a hard drive from scratch. Everything they learn in the classroom has a direct connection to a real-world career application. Even if they decide not to pursue careers in engineering or IT, they have built a repertoire of knowledge and skills—tools and resources to rely on in the future. Most important, these experiences help students to understand why they are in school and how their hard work is helping them to prepare for college or a career.

Families and caregivers also see the value of the career academies for motivating their students. One parent of a 10th-grade student explained that he chose the school for his son because of its focus on mathematics and engineering. The engineering courses have since helped his son decide on a career path, which is to become a car designer. The parent credited the engineering academy's courses with helping his son to develop a vision for his future and to stay motivated to achieve his career goals.

MARBLE HILL HIGH SCHOOL

Marble Hill perceives fluency in more than one language as a great asset—not just for the student, but also for the entire school and community at large. As such, the school requires that *all* enrolled students learn a second or third language, including English for ELs, and Japanese, Chinese, or Italian for English Proficient students. The school structures support this through specific programming that places students in heterogeneous, multicultural, and multilingual settings while making use of extended instructional time and creative scheduling. To prepare students for college and career, the school also offers multiple opportunities within school and outside of school to prepare for postsecondary success. As such, it is evident that the school organizes its structures deliberately to support its mission as a school for international studies and help realize its goals for students.

Targeted Learning Environments for Diverse Students

There are two main programs at Marble Hill: the International program for English Proficient students, and the ESL program for English learners.

Incoming 9th- and 10th-grade English Proficient students are placed in either an Italian or Chinese strand (depending on which is offered at time of enrollment), or a Japanese strand. Meanwhile, incoming freshmen and sophomore English learners are placed in either a newcomer, SIFE, or beginner strand or in an intermediate and advanced ESL strand. The four strands allow school staff to strategically target supports and services to meet student needs and to build a community of students. There is a strong, schoolwide alignment across the strands to support inquiry, project-based learning, and other teaching practices.

All students take classes in the same subject areas during their freshman and sophomore years. (Only students who have already taken a certain class are exempt from this rule.) Marble Hill additionally requires that all students, including English Proficient ones, enroll in a second language. EL students, however, must take English as their second language. This setup allows ELs to potentially take two periods of English during their freshman and sophomore years. They also receive two English credits for the required and elective English classes. English Proficient students, meanwhile, have a choice between Japanese, Chinese, or Italian (depending on offerings). Staff commented on the fact that ELs are often motivated to pass their English exams so that they can be reclassified as English Proficient because they are excited to enroll in Italian, Chinese, or Japanese classes.

During 9th and 10th grades, students tend to move through courses together as cohort groups. For example, beginner ELs in the ESL program are placed in classes with other ELs throughout the day so that they receive support tailored specifically to their individual needs. Advanced and intermediate ELs similarly travel together in a cohort group for all academic classes, although they are mixed with English Proficient students for art and physical education. Assistant Principal Dingman shared:

> The goal is to give those ESL kids two super solid years of language instruction plus sheltered content instruction. In their first two years—except for classes like art, gym, and advisory—their content classes are with other ELs.

The aim is that students will have built up enough English language skills that they are able to participate in a class with English Proficient students in the later years. Thus, depending on their proficiency level, by junior year ELs are typically mixed in with English Proficient students in content classes such as history or science. However, some upperclassmen ELs may still be in ELA/ESL classes, while other ELs may be in a mixed ELA course with English Proficient students. A student commented on the program structure:

I like the fact that being an ESL student, when you start in 9th grade, it's only ESL students. You feel more comfortable being in a class with students who don't speak English just like you, instead of being mixed with those kids who are fluent in English and make you feel uncomfortable. . . . So they place ESL students together until 11th grade . . . when they mix everybody altogether.

Within 11th- and 12th-grade classes, students are placed in heterogeneous groups at the beginning of the year. Teachers then adjust these groups strategically throughout the year. School leadership always asks questions about grouping and placement decisions during class observations, and through professional learning teachers come to consider language scaffolding every time they group students. A teacher commented, "It's really something that we are taught to think about every time we do our groupings."

Marble Hill implements a "looping" model, which allows teachers to instructionally follow a group of students for a set number of years (Grant, 1996). Originally, this practice began in 2002 and 2003 within the history and English departments. It soon developed with the foreign language teachers as well, who currently follow a cohort of students for up to three years. The foreign language looping model proved to work so well that the principal was "floored with what the students [were] doing by year three," and the school decided to expand the model to other content areas in subsequent years. School leadership has always recognized the value of having teachers loop with students.

Decisions about looping, however, are not taken lightly. Careful planning goes into the decisionmaking process when determining which content areas and which teachers to include in the model. The principal explained:

Sometimes we don't loop, because of a certain teacher's strength with a group of students. . . . We have teachers that are particularly fantastic content teachers working with [EL] students, and specifically our [beginner EL] students. . . . We are not going to have a teacher teach our [beginner] EL students if they are not strong with them.

Additionally, the school ensures that teachers who participate in the looping model receive multiple professional learning opportunities and support. Typically, new teachers are not assigned to participate in the model. Instead they are given two to three years to prepare and adjust. School leadership believes that when teachers have to change things too much every year (as is often necessary with a looping model), it leads to teacher burnout. In this sense, the school supports and nurtures its teachers to ensure that they can provide the best instruction possible.

Extended Learning Time

Students at Marble Hill attend eight periods per day, which allows for extra instructional time. By extending the school day, all students receive the added support they need to learn language and content skills. In 9th and 10th grades, students have double periods of the same content class as needed. For instance, some students attend back-to-back Algebra classes taught by one teacher. This structure allows the teachers to slow down and go in depth. Figure 6.1 is a sample class schedule for freshmen students, either in the ESL or International program. Every student also has an advisory period.

Resources Organized to Create a Supportive Learning Environment

The school has recently hired a full-time college advisor with grant money from the College Bound Initiative (CBI), a partner organization that empowers youth to achieve success beyond high school. This partnership has helped expose Marble Hill students to more opportunities. For example, the school hosts two college fairs a year with 59 colleges and college representatives who come to present and talk with students. The school also offers Saturday test preparation programs for students, as well as college-level courses in psychology and sociology. Other opportunities to enroll in on-campus college courses during junior and senior year are made available through the College Now program in partnership with Lehman College.

One of the key features of the CBI program is a College Readiness Class (CRC) for 12th-graders. In the first semester of their senior year, students take a one-hour course, four days a week, in which they research colleges; write college research papers, essays, and personal statements; apply for

Figure 6.1. Sample Freshman Year Courses

MONDAY, TUESDAY, THURSDAY, FRIDAY

- Humanities—1 hour 30 min
- Algebra or Geometry—1 hour 30 min
- English/ESL—1 hour
- Environmental Science—1 hour
- Foreign Language or ESL—1 hour
- Physical Education—1 hour 40 min (2 days/week)

WEDNESDAY (SHORTENED DAY)

- Advisory
- Art, Drama, Dance, or Film
- Health

financial aid; and assemble college applications. College representatives attend the class regularly to answer questions and help students make decisions about where to apply. The program prompts students to question their future and the role education will play in it. It also helps students navigate the college application process. One student shared that they visit colleges, even those that are out of state.

There is also a College Seminar, which consists of an exit project focused on preparing students for college by having them conduct research, prepare résumés, and reflect on their educational trajectory. The Senior Exit Project occurs in the form of an interview process, but it is geared around college. Students must submit an explanation about the college selections they made, a college-level English paper, a community service paper, and a personal essay as progress markers in their college application process.

Students are also encouraged to enroll in the variety of Advanced Placement courses offered by the school, and they are aware and appreciative of the extensive support behind them to ensure that they achieve their college and career goals. One student said, "Different high schools have different policies . . . Some of them don't even do the Regents . . . no projects. I wonder how they pass their classes." Another student observed, "You get to have great teachers, who help you, who make you go to college, who are always motivating you."

NEW WORLD HIGH SCHOOL

The instructional program at New World is designed and distinguished by structures that converge to ensure that all students are exposed to rigorous college preparatory content while simultaneously obtaining English language proficiency. Characterized by a looping model where teachers follow a cohort of students throughout their high school career, New World also uses specific student grouping and assessment approaches that allow staff to design the best instructional program for each student. Additionally, many of the academic supports are built into the structure of the day and are embedded in the everyday practices of the school.

Targeted Learning Environments for Diverse Students

A fundamental element of New World's instructional model involves looping, an approach that enables teachers to assume a cohort of students in 9th grade and stay with them until graduation. Although there are some scheduling challenges—for example, 11th- and 12th-graders may need to take different Advanced Placement courses and therefore may have different teachers—all students generally have the same content teachers all four years. This system allows for an extraordinary sense of consistency and accountability. Since teachers stay with their students year after year, they know the students well and take full responsibility for each student's learning. When discussing looping, one teacher shared:

> It gives us an opportunity to really get to know our students. We know their strengths and weaknesses. And we know what happened in previous years in terms of curriculum. I know exactly what they didn't get to. I know exactly what I might have skipped last year.

Another teacher related how the model facilitates classroom management and allows for teachers and students to develop trusting relationships. One teacher stated, "We get to know them, but they also get to know us. They really form a bond with you. . . . If they come here from another country, it can be so overwhelming. But this [looping] is something that is consistent for them." For ELs, forming a trusting bond with a teacher can be a source of motivation for participating in classroom discussions. Likewise, teachers can develop better lessons that are more aligned with the needs of each student.

Recognizing that credit accumulation is an issue for many ELs who want to attend college, New World meets the academic needs of its students through its unique instructional arrangement. For example, students take more than the required courses so that they have multiple opportunities to succeed and not fall behind in acquiring their required graduation credits. New World has a block schedule, with nine periods a day and almost seven hours of daily instructional time, and academic supports are embedded throughout the instructional day. All 9th- and 10th-grade students are required to take an extra class in English and math. Core subject teachers of English, math, and science teach these double periods, and the setup is intended to provide additional support via instructional time for all students while also leaving room for electives, such as art or dance. The principal explained the rationale behind this added support so that students do not have to go into credit recovery mode (i.e., when students fail or want to retake a course or have not taken a required course for graduation):

> We are spending a lot of time in credit recovery and a lot of money on credit recovery. So instead of having credit recovery, I give them extra classes now. This will give them better options. Later on, I don't have to put that much money in credit recovery. I'm taking that money and using it to hire extra teachers. This also gives me less of a need for after-school tutoring. I'm taking that money and putting it to the extra period. I don't need that much summer school.

A period for advisory is also a core element of the schedule, geared at providing support for college and career readiness. Beginning in 9th grade, advisory is used to help students develop academic, personal, and social skills for success. Basic skills such as note-taking, social skills, navigating the school, and acclimating to the culture of New World are emphasized in the earlier grades. College counselors regularly visit the classes to inform students about colleges, internships, and other opportunities. In the later years, the emphasis is on college applications. Advisory typically consists of one 45-minute period a week, though there is flexibility. Some students take a 90-minute period while others opt out, depending on their needs. The curriculum for advisory used to be based on a program called "American Dream," but this has evolved over the years and the school has instead developed a program based on experiences with past cohorts.

For struggling students, academic interventions play an important role in ensuring a personalized approach for each child. New World employs the use of a targeted intervention system in which a team of counselors, teachers, and administrators share data on student progress to monitor interventions. The system involves families in the process to help them be aware of the strengths and weaknesses of their children. These academic interventions let students know what is expected of them to demonstrate improvement. Working collaboratively, counselors and teachers meet for case conferences during grade-level meetings to talk about what is and is not working for a student. The aim of these meetings is to figure out how to support the student academically and socially. Recommendations may include referrals to the school's Saturday Academy for extra academic support or even to the Health Clinic so that students' physical and mental well-being are provided for.

Recognizing the importance of collaboration time for teachers of ELs, New World provides plenty of opportunities for teacher collaboration by department and grade level. During common planning time, teachers are expected to examine student work together, share activities with one another, present lessons to the team, and reflect on their instructional practices. The goal is to enable teachers to share their expertise, and to integrate disciplinary knowledge with language development to enhance ELs' academic performance.

To ensure that effective teacher collaboration takes place, the staff carves out common planning time for teachers twice a week on Mondays and Tuesdays. This time is split between department and grade-level teams. During this collaboration time, teachers develop rubrics, which can vary by grade and English proficiency levels. Many of the rubrics are based on the Regents exams, but they are also developed and modified by teams of teachers who work together. Generally, collaboration time gives teachers the space to reflect on their practice or to create new instructional and evaluative tools as a departmental or grade-level team. One teacher reflected on the experience of collaboration and its effect on teacher practice:

> We as English teachers work very closely with the [administrative and support] staff. We talk about the language. . . . We meet with various teachers by grade level. We also do inter-visitations where we see other subject areas. We also examine student work . . . [There are] all kinds of interactions between the staff. We talk about language. If we are having trouble with an idea or a concept, we ask, "What kind of vocabulary are you using? How are you structuring your sentences?" Between the English and Social Studies department, we are trying to be more consistent with the language that we use for the essays.

In this sense, the common planning time is used to help teachers grow professionally by encouraging them to reflect on their practice and identify areas of growth to improve student learning. Assistant Principal Gashi shared that it also "promotes trust and ownership in teacher teams." Teachers are given the opportunity to become leaders and gain deeper understanding of their practice.

Resources Organized to Create a Supportive Learning Environment

A major focus for New World is ensuring that students are prepared for success in college and career. The school proudly announces that it is geared toward preparing immigrant students for an academic trajectory, even if students are undocumented. The university counselor stated their expectations clearly:

> We are very college-focused. We say that from day one—in fact, when we have 8th-graders coming to visit the school, we say, "We are a college-focused school. If that doesn't feel right to you, you may want to look at other schools because we will push you and prepare you for university."

The school offers abundant resources to ensure that this vision of college and career readiness is met. One of the resources New World provides is an SAT preparation course. This service is provided through the school's partnership with Fordham University, and is specially customized for the needs of New World High School. One network administrator discussed the service, saying, "We have supported the school as an organization through offering Kaplan services for SAT [support]. We met with staff and the administration so that we could tailor the program specifically to the needs of students."

New World also has a full-time university counselor who helps students with a range of college preparation activities. Her duties include helping students with college application requirements, organizing an advanced writing class for 11th-graders to work on writing their Common Application essay, letting students know about graduation and college requirements, organizing college visits, assisting students and families with financial aid applications, and generally providing academic counseling for all students. She spends time setting goals with each individual student and regularly visits classes to ensure that students are on track to get into college. Students report that there is abundant help with applying to college and that they constantly receive email reminders to submit materials by deadlines. One student expressed that it was helpful to have relationships between professors and students explained to them, and that she enjoyed listening to alumni come back to answer questions about college life.

CONCLUSION

Creating an organizational structure that supports ELs' progress is central to a high school's success. The components of this design element include: (1) resources organized to create a supportive learning environment, (2) extended learning time, and (3) targeted learning environments for ELs.

Resources to create a supportive learning environment involve flexibility within the master schedule and in course options. At the High School for Dual Language and Asian Studies, for example, the guidance and instructional teams work closely to determine students' needs and then design courses to maximize students' learning opportunities. This may mean creating a section for ESL-Biology if demand exists. With respect to extended learning time, High School for Dual Language and Asian studies, like many of the schools, is open on Saturdays for college prep courses, physical education, and workshops in ELD and SAT preparation. Marble Hill, by contrast, provides extended learning time by requiring students to attend eight periods per day. By extending the school day, all students receive the added support they need to hone both knowledge of language and content. An example of providing a targeted learning environment for ELs is also found at Marble Hill, where all 9th- and 10th-graders are required to take classes in the same subject areas, including one class in a foreign language. For ELs, their ESL course counts as their foreign language. Therefore, every EL in 9th and 10th grades takes two periods of English every semester. Further allowing them more personalized instruction is the practice of moving 9th- and 10th-graders through their courses together with ELs of the same or similar English proficiency level. This pays dividends in their junior and senior years when they are mixed into heterogeneous cohorts with more proficient peers.

The next chapter examines the seventh and final design element of successful schools for ELs—strategic family and community partnerships.

CHAPTER 7

Design Element 7

Strategic Family and Community Partnerships

> I love the [school], activities, travel, everything they offer. . . . The teachers and the patience they have taken with each one [of my kids]. . . . No school is superior. I am grateful that they gave me notice and worked with me . . . but I have even more appreciation because they have opened my eyes to how to help [my kids]. . . . My daughter is in a college program now. (a Marble Hill parent sharing her recognition of the effectiveness of the school's approach)

Through the enactment of the innovative design elements described in the previous chapters, the schools we studied have created places of learning that push students to high levels of academic success while supporting them each step of the way. However, the schools have not achieved this alone. Instead, they have leaned on strong ties with the local community and the families of their students as allies in their work (Bryk, 2010; Epstein, 2001; Henderson & Mapp, 2002; Jeynes, 2007). School teams view parents and caregivers as crucial allies and take extensive measures to involve families in their students' education. At many of the schools, family liaisons who speak the families' native language or come from similar cultural backgrounds make families feel at ease and more empowered to engage with their child's education.

Across these schools, parents and caregivers hold high expectations for their children and see college as a means to success in the United States. However, for many families in these school communities, college for their children may seem like an unreachable goal because of background experiences and life circumstances. These schools believe that collaborating closely with families and community-based organizations is essential to providing students with a full range of supports and opportunities.

Schools have also forged lasting partnerships with external organizations that are purposefully and carefully selected to augment and improve the existing practices at the school. The schools work strategically with these community organizations to expand opportunities for students. For example, the schools leverage the community partnerships to bolster the academic and extracurricular opportunities they offer to students. Many partner with local colleges and universities to offer college-level courses, so that students often graduate with college credits. Other partnerships provide mentoring or internship opportunities to students to expand their social capital. Another area in which these schools have leveraged external partnerships to further student success is to provide intensive college counseling and guidance. These partnerships supplement the support students receive from their schools through college visits, application support, and mentorships.

External providers and outside organizations also support these schools in growing their vision and building their organizational capacity. The partners offer support services that a district or school may not be capable of providing, such as professional learning opportunities, instructional coaching for teachers, or leadership coaching for administrators. Navigating the array of services available to schools and districts, however, can often be a daunting task. Outside organizations may suggest practices that are not aligned with the vision of the school, and partnerships can go awry for a variety of reasons. This chapter highlights ways school teams have successfully leveraged and adapted partnerships with external organizations so that the services are aligned to the school's mission and vision.

Within the design element of family and community partnerships, the essential components include:

- **Open Communications with Students' Families.** Schools acknowledge their own strengths and limitations and are willing to engage in meaningful conversations and actions toward improvements in student learning. This includes involving families in the caring and learning work, while respecting their unique and diverse experiences.
- **Strategic Selection of Partnerships.** Schools coordinate with professional learning partners and community-based organizations so that the appropriate resources and opportunities are available to students, their families, and the school.

This chapter spotlights how three schools initiate and manage the design components of family and community partnerships for the benefit of their ELs' academic achievements.

MARBLE HILL HIGH SCHOOL

At Marble Hill, leaders and staff recognize that partnering with families is a crucial component in ensuring that students meet high expectations for college and career success. Typically involved in everything from attendance, dress code, and diversity to college preparation, parents and caregivers report feeling welcomed as a part of the school. Marble Hill has been able to maintain positive relationships with families to work as a team in helping their students succeed.

External partnerships also play a major role in the success of Marble Hill. Their "network partner," the New Visions network, provides support in terms of data analysis and through access to numerous services. In addition, partnerships with outside organizations focused on college and career help Marble Hill achieve its goals for students.

Open Communications with Students' Families

Because Marble Hill has been identified as a top school in the Bronx in recent years, the parent population is changing to include middle-class, well-educated families in addition to the many immigrant families with little formal education or English proficiency. Balancing these dynamics is at times challenging for school staff. They sometimes face difficulties in reaching out to the non-English-speaking families, but they overcome this barrier by hiring translators, creating a welcoming environment, and providing support for all families. For example, to address language barriers, they have a staff who speak Spanish, Bengali, Urdu, and several African languages, and they frequently use the New York City Department of Education's phone translation services, specifically for some African languages. The school taps their students for help with translation, which has an added advantage of helping families see how valuable it is to speak more than one language. One staff member commented that, "When [parents and caregivers] come in, they are surprised by the fact that the principal speaks three different dialects and [the assistant principal] speaks different languages, too. They are impressed by that, and they feel even more welcome. . . ."

In addition to full-school events that acknowledge and celebrate diversity such as International Dinner night, where families share their dishes and dress in traditional garb, Marble Hill provides workshops for families on a variety of topics, such as drugs, bullying, immigration, ESL, graduation, college, and financial aid. In the spirit of maintaining open communication with families, the school hosts frequent parent-teacher conferences, sends parent newsletters in preferred languages, and hosts an online grading and homework site. The principal makes it a goal to call five parents and caregivers a day to check in as a way of encouraging ongoing trust and engagement in school activities.

In describing Marble Hill's school culture of camaraderie with families, one parent explained, "The [staff] here always has an open door for you and they make themselves available at any time to respond and give us the best advice. . . . When I least expect it, I am visiting the teachers, the principal, the counselors. . . . I am a personal friend [of the staff]."

Strategic Selection of Partnerships

Marble Hill, like many schools in New York, works with an external "network partner" that provides a particularly high level of support—the New Visions network. New Visions helps Marble Hill analyze data about students and provides access to numerous services, including an online grading system, a math program (Silicon Valley Math Initiative), and extended opportunities for ELs through the iMentor program. The principal explained, "We get a lot of value from New Visions. They provide innovative data and information systems . . . [and] they provide professional development and wonderful data tools."

New Visions for Public Schools (www.newvisions.org) is a Partnership Support Organization serving 70 public schools across New York City. The organization's aim is to provide support to educators by providing "the tools and training they need to analyze student performance, diagnose problems and design solutions to improve instruction." New Visions works with school staff and community organizations to provide ambitious, rigorous instruction and to design curricula that are relevant to students' lives and aligned to college and job skills.

Marble Hill's relationship with New Visions has shifted over the years. Since partnering together, New Visions has assigned a School Support Facilitator (SSF) to help Marble Hill with curriculum development, classroom observations, instruction, and feedback on sustainable practices. For example, New Visions has trained Marble Hill leaders in conducting observations using the Danielson framework (2011). The SSF has also served as a broker of resources, helping the school find sources of funding for professional learning services, such as the Sheltered Instruction Observation Protocol (SIOP), Quality Teaching for English Learners (QTEL) training, iMentor, and the Open Educational Resources (OER) collection of curriculum materials.

In more recent years, however, the focus of the support has shifted more toward the effective use of data. More specifically, New Visions helps the school look at individual student patterns and holds strategic data check-ins to identify students at risk of graduation. The principal explained that the role of New Visions is more focused on:

> understanding the systems that the [Department of Education]
> has already, understanding the inaccuracies of that system and the
> inefficiencies of it. One big shift they have made . . . is looking at
> how those data systems really shift what we do in schools to make
> our work that much more effective with the end goal of making sure
> students get to graduation. . . . They look at things like programming.
> How are you programming? How are you providing the appropriate

classes? Or making sure you are [providing appropriate classes]. Really having systems where that data is accessible . . . and where you can manipulate it enough to determine what is needed.

With these supports, Marble Hill leverages opportunities to ensure that they efficiently achieve their school goals.

In addition to the partnership with New Visions, Marble Hill contracts with many other outside groups, some through paid partnerships and others through the affiliation with New Visions. These collaborations are geared toward offering opportunities for students to prepare for college and career success. For example, College Now offers students the opportunity to enroll in college-level courses and earn college credit at Lehman College while still in high school, and Changing the Odds is a youth development project offered by the Morris Heights Health Center, with the aim of engaging youth in healthy behaviors and helping them learn life skills. Other partners include Dream Yard (focused on drawing, dance, and poetry as extracurricular activities), Minds Matter (a college preparatory program for high-achieving students), and the South Bronx Action Group.

Collectively, these partnerships and services support Marble Hill in achieving its mission of helping students develop the necessary skills to "acquire and apply knowledge." By selecting these partnerships in a strategic way that is aligned with its vision, Marble Hill has been able to maintain a strong focus on its goals while still obtaining support from external partners. Assistant Principal Dingman stated, "We realize that we cannot do this alone. We work with many other organizations to support our ELs."

MANHATTAN BRIDGES HIGH SCHOOL

At Manhattan Bridges, the staff establishes clear relationships with local community organizations to build local capacity and augment student learning opportunities. A student summed up the wealth of opportunities at Manhattan Bridges in the following way: "Our school, they . . . want you to be successful in high school, be successful in college, be successful in life. That's the basic goal."

A prime example of these opportunities is Manhattan Bridges' partnership with Cornell University's Hydroponics Program and Internship, where student interns are paid to work after school with a university professor to conduct research on growing lettuce, cabbages, and fish at the forefront of sustainable science. One student intern proudly shared that the salad and fish served in the school cafeteria come from the hydroponics program. Because she is interested in science, the opportunity to take part in the hydroponics research has given her a preview into the work that scientists do.

Beyond this, the program has also given her a taste of what it is like to be a college student.

The Hydroponics Program is one of the many partnerships Manhattan Bridges has forged with organizations outside the school to provide students with opportunities to stretch their high school experience. Through a partnership with College Now at The City University of New York, students take College 101 and courses in psychology and criminal justice at the John Jay College of Criminal Justice, allowing them to graduate from high school with up to 16 college credits. Summer programs at St. Joseph's College New York and Fordham University provide students with SAT preparation, and the Options Center at Goddard Riverside Community Center gives students additional one-on-one college counseling. Students also speak enthusiastically about the many opportunities available to them to take part in job shadowing experiences at companies such as Verizon, Juniper, AT&T, Ernst & Young, and American Express. Professionals from Verizon and Juniper come to campus to work with students on their résumés and coach them in their personal and professional learning. These powerful out-of-school experiences with industry professionals help to expose students to new career fields and allow them to see the connection between what they are learning in school and their future goals.

Beyond these opportunities to extend students' learning, Manhattan Bridges has also sought to provide students with adult role models. Through a far-reaching partnership with the organization iMentor, students in 9th, 10th, and 11th grades have been matched to professional mentors from across New York City. Mentors meet with their mentees during monthly events and provide another layer of support to help students focus on their college and career goals. Students and their families alike value the wealth of opportunities available for helping students to explore their goals. One parent credits the iMentor program with helping her son to find a vision for his future and become more motivated to overcome the obstacles in his way.

NEW WORLD HIGH SCHOOL

Recognizing that the school must work in collaboration with families to ensure college and career readiness, New World makes a significant effort to reach out to them with the goal of involving them in the school experience. The principal noted, "In terms of outside support, it [requires] extensive counseling and outreach. I meet with 90–95% of the families once their kids come to my school. . . . Right [from] the beginning, I tell them, 'This school is different than other schools, and this is what we are going to expect.'" It is this persistent, insistent, and consistent relationship that the school has with their students' families that creates a tight-knit partnership throughout the students' high school journey at New World.

Open Communications with Students' Families

One of the main ways in which the school connects with parents and caregivers is by ensuring positive and consistent communication. By maintaining a welcoming environment for families from the very first interactions with New World, the staff maintains strong and trusting relationships. For example, the school admissions secretary mentioned, "It's very interesting when we don't speak the same language yet we are all on the same page. It works. And I think it works because of our rapport, our happiness, and our willingness to help these students."

Furthermore, the school makes a concerted effort to make phone calls to parents and caregivers every single day in the language of choice. New World has interpreters in most languages through a service provided by the city's Department of Education. Teachers also have one period each Wednesday for parent outreach. One teacher shared, "We call home all the time. The office calls, we call home, we log when we call home. . . . We all know when something is wrong. And we all try to help the students." As evidence of the incredibly high expectations that New World sets not just for students but also families, one parent recounted her experience with the school's outreach: "They call or send a letter before an event. Most of the time they call . . . If my daughter is even a minute late, they call." The increased attention on attendance and tardiness relates directly back to their mission of rigorous academic instruction—if students are not in school on time every day, then they are missing valuable learning time.

Family outreach, however, is not without its challenges. Staff members spoke of cultural barriers that needed to be addressed. An administrator explained some of the parent interactions, saying, "We met with the parents— some parents were a little uncomfortable with having students going out of the borough . . . There is a cultural context. So we alleviated concerns by answering questions." A support member of the staff emphasized the importance of constant follow-up: "Parents work a lot, some have more than one job, so it is difficult for them to come to school. So we call them. We follow up if they don't respond."

Strategic Selection of Partnerships

New World has been able to sustain effective partnerships by respecting the work of their partners and by maintaining a sharp focus on their mission. They collaborate with outside organizations, including Fordham University's Graduate School of Education, College Now, and the New York City Leadership Academy, among others. The focus of their partnerships is always on improving the quality of instruction, with targeted support for individual teachers. New World's work with external partners helps to bolster their vision for preparing ELs for success in college and careers.

Since 2007, New World has been working in collaboration with Fordham University through the Center for Educational Partnerships. As explained on the Fordham website, this partnership is "dedicated to applying . . . research in the service of K–12 teachers, administrators, students, and families, as well as to education and government agencies to enable all children to achieve and succeed academically."

According to one of the network administrators, this is a "very different way of a university working with a school. It is not the usual placement of student teachers and/or graduate fellows." Instead, this partnership is geared toward providing a wide range of support services for the school. The network's relationship with New World involves academic support and nonacademic human resources budgeting. Fordham's role is extensive—they have provided guidance and financial supports related to transportation, building location, space utilization, professional learning, compliance, and data systems training. Essentially, the network helps with whatever is necessary to strengthen the "unique design" of the school.

Most notable is how New World has leveraged this partnership to provide targeted instructional support for teachers and help with curriculum design. One Fordham administrator reflected, "They [already] had [developed] their curriculum, and they really knew what they wanted to do. So I will not and cannot take credit for that . . . but, to help it be successful? That is when we would come in." In collaboration with New World administrators, Fordham conducts conferences with school leadership to define areas of need. As one example, in the early years of the school, when the principal noticed that the science program needed to be refined, Fordham worked closely with leaders and teachers to improve science curriculum and instruction. The partner helped hire science teachers and recommended a retired science teacher to serve as a coach and mentor to the staff as they developed the new science initiative. The coach observed classrooms, provided feedback, and met with teachers to infuse better strategies.

In later years, instructional specialists and coaches were expanded to all content areas as needed. Since coaches are not at the school every day, staff at the school provide guidelines to them on how to support teachers. The current structure, according to Assistant Principal Gashi, includes having the coaches meet "with teachers to review and discuss what the teachers plan to teach, followed by classroom visits, and debriefing to reflect and plan for next steps." He believes that this structure has been the best way to help teachers improve their practice.

New World also works very closely with numerous organizations to provide professional learning for faculty and administrators, and college and career opportunities as well as health services for students. One such organization is the New York City Leadership Academy, which is a nonprofit organization that helps to prepare educators to "lead schools that accelerate student learning" and that increases the "capacity of systems across the country to develop and support" educational leaders. Another partnership that provides professional learning services is Lehman College. New World is part of Lehman College's professional learning network.

Meanwhile, the College Now program provides other opportunities for college and career readiness by offering college classes to juniors and seniors on the City University of New York campus as well as college prep programs to coach students through the application process. New World served as a pilot site for online college courses through CUNY's School of Professional Studies, and the school continues to offer courses through this program. Additionally, New World serves as a hub center for Lehman College to train Noyce Scholars—a scholarship funded by the National Science Foundation that supports students in obtaining bachelor's and master's degrees in STEM fields. The Changing the Odds program at the Morris Heights Health Center is a school-based health center focused on developing life skills, and works closely with New World to address the social-emotional needs of their students.

Once New World has partnered with an organization, the school maintains positive relations with external partners by being communicative and remaining open to feedback. Outside organizations report feeling valued and welcomed at the school. One external provider noted, "The administrators are very cooperative and receptive. They are not defensive. They listen and try it out." Meanwhile, another provider shared, "It's an incredibly organized school . . . there's an incredible sense of trust among all three [leaders] as well as their teaching staff. That's why when you suggest something to teachers, they don't take it as an offense—they look at it as a way to try new things."

Despite the high number of partnerships with outside organizations, New World maintains a level of programmatic coherence that allows them to avoid getting derailed with interventions and services that are not in accordance with their mission. As previously mentioned, the New World leaders serve as liaisons between the outside organizations and the school to make sure that there is close alignment between the services provided by the partners and the needs of the school.

CONCLUSION

An essential design element in all of the schools we studied is a close collaboration with families, community-based partners, and (at times) external organizations to provide students with a full array of supports and opportunities. Many schools, for example, partner with local colleges and universities to offer students college-level courses. Other partnerships are forged to provide intensive college counseling and guidance. Components that are essential in the formation and maintenance of these partnerships include: (1) open communication with students' families, and (2) the strategic selection of partnerships.

New World High School connects with parents and caregivers by ensuring positive and consistent communication. One of the ways in which the school creates a welcoming environment for families is by communicating with families in the language of their choice. Working with the interpreting service offered by the New York City Department of Education, New World is able to provide interpreters in most languages. The school is quick to communicate with families about general information like school events and also individual information like student absences. Such frequent communication is important to building trust between the school and parent community.

Manhattan Bridges illustrates how strategic partnerships assist ELs in becoming college- and career-ready. In addition to partnering with St. Joseph's College New York and Fordham University to provide students with SAT preparation in the summer, Manhattan Bridges also works with outside individuals to provide students with opportunities to take part in job shadowing experiences at a variety of companies. Professionals from various industries come to campus to work with students on their résumés and coach them in their personal and professional learning.

Together all seven design principles described in the preceding chapters contribute to the success of each high school. In our concluding chapter, we highlight the importance of building upon shared values.

CHAPTER 8

Building an Infrastructure Based on Shared School Values

The schools presented in this book offer new insights into the design elements we described in Chapters 1–7. We found that when implemented across schools, these features support successful development of English proficiency and high levels of academic achievement among ELs. From their inception, the founders of these schools began with a clear vision of and singular focus on improving the educational outcomes of ELs, building into each school a "can-do" attitude accompanied by the establishment of unique practices that when refined over time have yielded extraordinary results. The practices employed in these schools are not only essential for ELs' success but, as the performance data show, they also benefit *all* students. By attending to ELs, these schools create an environment such that all students can excel, especially those who are low-income and otherwise traditionally outside of the sphere of academic success.

In addition to identifying the design elements of these schools, we found that they shared six values, which we listed in the Introduction to this book. These values guide the schools' daily actions and decisionmaking and shape how students and their families have experienced the schools. In this closing chapter, we explore the schools' enactment of each value, which collectively creates an inclusive school culture that supports the growth of all ELs. We conclude with a challenge for educators nationwide.

VALUE 1:
The School Puts Forth an Ambitious Mission Focused on Preparing All Students for College and Career Success

From the moment students walk through the door of the schools we studied, it is conveyed to them repeatedly that they can and will succeed. This mindset goes beyond "high expectations"—the school makes a commitment to prepare every single student for postsecondary education, and ensures that students will not need remediation once they are there. The school stops at nothing to make this happen: instruction is rigorous, and an extremely high level of support helps students to meet this level of rigor.

This preparation toward college and careers is operationalized through a deliberate focus on the strengths and interests of each student, and creating pathways with rigorous coursework for accelerated learning during the student's high school career. First, each school leads with vision, belief, and actions that prepare every student for college and career success, and for responsible, civically engaged citizenship in their local community and the world.

Each school's mission encapsulates ideas, images, and goals that are embodied by the community of learners and leaders. These schools' missions serve as clear beacons guiding members of the school community as they work deliberately and incrementally each day to nourish students' language and cultural diversities, set ambitious goals, and help students master rigorous college-preparatory coursework as they progress toward greater opportunities and aspirations.

The missions across the six schools embrace the language and cultural diversities of their students and leverage these assets to motivate and accelerate both day-to-day learning and cultivate lifelong learners. For example, explicit in the school's mission and vision at Dual Language, Manhattan Bridges, and Marble Hill is the imperative to prepare students to be fully bilingual and biliterate in two languages. At the High School for Dual Language and Asian Studies, all students study Chinese and English concurrently over the course of their academic careers (see Chapter 1). At the Marble Hill School for International Studies, the school community sees fluency in more than one language as a great asset—not just for the student, but also for the entire school and community at large. Here, all students learn a second or third language of their choosing. This includes English for ELs, and Japanese, Chinese, or Italian for English Proficient students (see Chapter 6). Across these sites, a major component of the school's mission is the belief that language development is a resource for all students, to be used in service of their learning and in their lives.

The schools' missions, paired with their explicit articulation of their goals and visions, also serve as a consistent motivator for students and teachers in their learning journey together. Over the course of students' high school careers, they grow to embrace and internalize an ethos of intrinsic motivation and work with their teachers to set high academic and career expectations so that they are prepared for postsecondary success. To spur students' development toward college and career readiness, teachers leverage external goals such as high school graduation and state testing mandates as markers of student progress. Each of the schools has raised the bar for their high school graduates beyond the minimum district and state mandates.

For example, at Marble Hill all students, including those with interrupted formal education, know that they are expected to learn English, pass the New York Regents State exams with high scores, and be accepted into a college of their choice. Similarly, at Dual Language, students are encouraged to aim for a high pass of 90 or more on the Regents exam to earn an Honors designation, above and beyond a mere passing score of 65 for a Regents Diploma. Finally, at Manhattan Bridges High School, students need to earn 54 credits to graduate, instead of the 44 credits typically required of high school students in New York City.

Lastly, these ambitious goalposts are also reflected in the daily teaching and learning work that occurs across the myriad of courses designed specifically to accelerate students' academic, social, and emotional development into young adulthood.

VALUE 2:
The School Mission Guides All Decisions

At each of the schools we studied, the mission is more than simply words on a wall; instead, it is embodied by the school community and enacted through the many decisions that shape the school's trajectory. Every aspect of the school experience is thoughtfully and intentionally designed in keeping with the mission, including

- The design and scheduling of courses
- The hiring of committed and qualified employees and supporting their professional learning
- The partnerships with community organizations

Absolutely no opportunity is wasted in moving the school closer to its goals.

For example, at New World, the leadership understands that high levels of programmatic coherence are necessary to achieve schoolwide goals. When asked about the most important elements for creating a successful program, Principal Salazar advised others to "look at the mission of the school . . . and do not deviate from it." Here, the school team recognized that credit accumulation was an issue for many EL students who want to attend college. To lessen and resolve this barrier for their students, New World utilizes block scheduling with nine periods a day and almost seven hours of daily instructional time, with supplementary English and math courses for all 9th- and 10th-grade students. Core subject-area teachers of English, math, and science provide additional support during these double periods for all students, and block scheduling allows time for students to take electives such as art and dance (see Chapter 6).

Similarly, at Marble Hill, the structures and design of the school are all intentionally organized to support an inquiry- and project-based approach to education aligned to their school mission and vision as a school for international studies. This begins with a proactive intake process to recruit a diverse student body of 50% ELs and 50% English Proficient students. As discussed in Chapter 6, Marble Hill also offers two different types of programs, the ESL and International strands, to target support and services to its diverse student body. Block scheduling and looping allow for increased instructional time, which in turn enables teachers and students to spend more time getting to know one another, and give teachers the opportunity to build depth, coherence, and continuity across lessons.

This laser-sharp focus on what is best for students in the school's decisionmaking is also explicit in Manhattan Bridges's theory of action. As Principal Sanchez-Medina explained:

> We're looking at the child and the needs of the child. What has really defined us is that we build the structure around the student, as opposed to pushing the kid into a particular structure. So every decision we're making, we're looking at: Who are our students? Where do we want them to be?

This approach of starting with the child, respecting individuality, and being open to different pathways to success is the guiding principle behind the extensive individualized programming that each student receives at Manhattan Bridges.

At the same time, the attention on students' development is matched by the deliberate recruitment, retention, and development of the teachers and staff, and community partnerships that augment and improve upon the existing practices at the school.

VALUE 3:
The School Community Holds a Mindset of Continuous Improvement

In the schools presented in this book, administrators, staff, teachers, and students reflect continuously on their practices as they strive to fulfill the mission of success for every student. This focus on continuous improvement aims to achieve quality outcomes in classrooms and schools by directly addressing the complexity and variability of learning in context (Bryk, Gomez, Grunow, & LeMahieu, 2015). With goals of accelerating progress, a school team gathers and reviews timely student data that allow the school to adapt its teaching and course structures to how students learn. This stance of continuous improvement extends into the classrooms, where we see both teachers and students taking charge of and reflecting on their own learning.

In Marble Hill's partnership with New Visions for Public Schools, a professional learning support provider, the school leadership and the teachers have focused their work toward more effective use of data (see Chapter 7). Together, they regularly review patterns of individual and group-level student data, hold strategic data check-ins to identify students at risk of not graduating, and modify the system of supports so that students can get back on track toward graduation and college. The use of data informs decision-making at the student level, and allows school teams to act flexibly in better supporting student development.

Meanwhile, at New World, staff embraces an action research agenda that is aligned with the core values of their school. As explained in Chapter 5, this form of professional learning is intended to promote ongoing critical examination of instruction among teachers wherein they are expected to test their own hypotheses of instructional practices and adjust those practices based on the results of their inquiry. These processes focus on teaching and learning, as well as on the social and cultural elements of the classroom that may impact outcomes for students, especially emerging ELs. Based upon their findings, teachers adjust their teaching and reflect further on the changes made. This schoolwide process supports growth for both teachers and students.

The ingrained culture of feedback and reflection is not lost on students at these schools. Across sites, there is a willingness to talk about areas of growth, embrace students of all language proficiencies, and provide opportunities for students to take risks, make mistakes, and learn from them. In classrooms that we observed, students' voices and ideas are heard frequently and in multiple languages. Students are not afraid to practice their English, knowing that their mistakes will help them grow. This value allows school leaders, staff, and students to test out their ideas, utilize a growth mindset for learning, and focus their actions toward continuous improvement, with the result of consistently raising the bar of success for students (Carnegie Foundation, 2017; David & Talbert, 2013).

VALUE 4:
The Entire School Community Shares Responsibility for Students' Success

Everyone in the schools we studied contributes significantly toward and takes responsibility for the success of every student. This includes staff members, network partners, families, and students themselves. Students know to ask for help when they need it and frequently help other students when they are struggling. The social and relational trust and respect among teachers, school leaders, families, and students contribute to the culture, climate, and interpersonal relationships within the school community (Bryk & Schneider, 2002). No matter how much power one individual has within the school, everyone within the school community is dependent on one another so they can work together and support one another's efforts toward shared goals.

A parent from Boston International High School and Newcomers Academy describes her son's relationship to his school in the following way:

I can see that my son is enthusiastic, likes to learn, likes to come to school, and feels like part of a community. Over time, my son has been able to communicate and work with others and they get together and are part of each other's lives.

At BINcA, parents and caregivers are considered a close-knit part of the extended school family, working hand-in-hand to support student and family academic and life success (see Chapter 3).

Across the schools, students described the important role that their teachers played in cultivating their sense of self-efficacy within and outside the school walls. The school teams take seriously their role as coaches and mentors to their students in building their personal life skills toolbox so that they can navigate and overcome challenges on their way to college and career success. An external community-based partner to New World noticed that the principal and assistant principals customized individual attention and support for each student (see Chapter 4).

Additionally, support staff indicated that school leaders organize their time and resources so that they can work directly with students and families, on top of regular meetings with counselors and teachers to support students' development. At Marble Hill, all administrators teach one class each semester in order to gain a deeper understanding of student and teacher needs and strengths.

Inside the classrooms, students take ownership and responsibility for their own learning. The expectations are clear and students are prepared to meet those goals. One student at Manhattan Bridges summarized the sentiment in the following way:

They push you . . . they won't let you just stay in the basic level. They want you to be the best you can . . . They know you're capable. . . . They're going to ask everything of you—that's their rule. . . . They asked for 100% of me.

VALUE 5:
The School Community Is Highly Attuned to Students' Needs and Capacities

Every detail of the academic environment at the schools in our study originates with the whole student—their family life, culture, and histories. Courses, schedules, and other structures are designed and adapted with the ever-changing student population in mind, including its array of unique language and cultural backgrounds and language proficiencies. The schools make no assumptions about the student body, but rather collect and analyze evidence on a day-to-day basis, as well as the long term, to inform decisions.

"High expectations, . . . extensive support, and putting students first," is how one teacher described the mantra of Manhattan Bridges High School. This powerful culture of commitment and belief that every student will succeed is based in both acknowledging and supporting their individual histories. Within this culture, students report feeling safe to take academic risks, and hold themselves accountable for their own learning (see Chapter 3).

Across each site, schools have created significant in- and out-of-school wraparound supports for newcomers and Students with Interrupted Formal Education. Site leaders along with the support team work closely with each student and their families in understanding their histories and needs. This includes intake interviews for new families, diagnostic assessments that gauge English and academic proficiencies, and ongoing progress monitoring so that students have the necessary tools to excel in school and in life.

For example, at BINcA, the Newcomers Academy is tailored specifically to the needs of SIFE. The instructional staff takes an additive bilingualism perspective and utilizes students' home languages to complement instruction, scaffold understanding of content knowledge, maximize student engagement, and facilitate learning in English (see Chapter 6). At New World, these newcomers are paired with ESL teachers three days a week after school for supplementary instruction, and all teachers receive extensive background information about incoming new arrivals and SIFE who are in their classrooms. An alumnus shared the following reflection during his time at New World:

> They really take the time to analyze who you are as a student, but they also take the time to know who you are as a human, and what are your experiences, so they can build on and know how to address you as an individual.

Meanwhile, at It Takes a Village Academy, students are offered emotional support through a well-developed and effective advisory program. With a student-to-advisor ratio of 10 to 1, this provides strong social-emotional support for struggling students (see Chapter 3).

VALUE 6:
There Is a Strong Sense of Pride in and Respect Toward All Cultures

The schools we studied value the diversity of students' languages and cultures and invest time and resources to understand the lived experiences of students. Students feel proud of their unique identities and abilities, and are guided to respect those of their peers as well.

Across the sites, schools employ a myriad of strategies that embrace and celebrate the wealth of linguistic and cultural diversities of their students, families, and staff. These strategies include schoolwide norms that allow students to connect to and creatively express their past histories and current experiences, recruitment of diverse staff and leadership, and welcoming families into the school community through regular and active outreach efforts.

In interviews across schools, students, families, and community partners frequently remarked on the cultural and language diversities represented by the school leadership, teachers, and staff. The mix of talents and experiences has been cultivated over time, and school leaders consider the recruitment of teachers as one of the top drivers in sustaining a strong and nurturing learning community for their students. For example, at Marble Hill, families are often surprised by the fact that the principal and the assistant principals speak multiple languages and dialects (see Chapter 7). At ITAVA, there is an overriding belief that students should see and interact with racially and ethnically diverse role models who have achieved success in both school and careers. Here, many teachers and staff members reflect the demographics and language groups represented at the school. Near the school entrance hangs a wall poster with pictures of school staff alongside information about their achievements, their diverse countries of origin, and the many languages they speak.

Lastly, each of the schools acknowledges that building relationships and trust with students' families works hand-in-hand with the mission and vision of the school. Whether that entails frequent and regular conversations with parents or caregivers regarding their child's progress, or larger annual events like the International Dinner hosted at Marble Hill (see Chapter 7), families know that the school is actively working to build a collaborative relationship with them. Even with additional staffing that supports family and community outreach efforts, the schools embrace the ethos that more could be done, and that they can always improve upon their current efforts in bringing students' families more actively into the school communities.

CONCLUSION

The schools in this book serve as models for the rest of the nation with their high educational outcomes. The challenge for educators who seek to emulate these schools is to completely reenvision the way in which programs for ELs are designed and supported. These students must be at the center of such improvement efforts. Schools must be designed or redesigned with consideration for *their* needs. Too frequently, schools force ELs to conform to an existing instructional model, built with a different population in mind.

Although the schools profiled in this book are small (each has fewer than 600 students enrolled), readers should not discount the relevance of our findings for larger, comprehensive high schools. We have highlighted numerous successful practices that most of these schools share and that, with careful planning and sufficient resources, can yield similar results in larger school contexts. To sum up, these schools

- Value cultural and linguistic diversity and leverage students' cultural and linguistic capital for learning;
- Deliberately hire and support staff with relevant backgrounds and experiences who are committed to ongoing development and growth and share the leadership's vision;
- Develop strong and unified language development frameworks that integrate language learning, literacy skills, subject-matter content, and analytical thinking;
- Benefit from the support of their districts and states, which creates the conditions that allow for tremendous innovation; and
- Partner with the community and with local colleges and universities to offer students a diverse array of academic and career-advancing supports.

The establishment of these and numerous other practices explored in this book is possible in *every* school, given a clear and focused vision and mission. The schools we describe serve as exemplars of what can be achieved when learning environments account for students' collective and individual needs and respond with practices and structures tailored to ensure students' success. What these schools demonstrate is that quality preparation for college and careers is not a privilege that is bestowed upon those fortunate enough to live in affluent communities and thriving economies. Rather, it can be available to *all* students when school communities are fully engaged and fully committed to enacting a clear, coherent, and equitable vision.

Methodology

SCHOOL SELECTION: MODELS WITH EFFECTIVE OUTCOMES

This study, conducted during the 2013–14 school year, sought to identify a small set of schools in the United States with highly effective outcomes for ELs and former ELs. Upon identification of these schools, our research questions were:

1. What are some high school models that have demonstrated strong academic and postsecondary outcomes for ELs?
2. How do school communities address the diversity of ELs across their classrooms and create learning environments that fully prepare students for colleges and careers?

Our team took multiple approaches in culling potential schools for this study. This included a systematic data analysis of college and career outcomes from key states and school districts in search of potential high schools with effective outcomes for ELs, as well as outreach and interviews with educators who work closely with ELs, and public nominations. We used a four-step process to identify schools:

1. Our research team identified the five school districts and 10 states with the highest EL enrollment, and the 10 states with the highest growth rates of ELs as determined by the National Center for Educational Statistics at the U.S. Department of Education (2017).
   a. For each of these districts and states, we examined all public high schools based on the following set of quantitative measures: EL graduation rate, EL college- and career-readiness (CCR) success indicators (i.e., college-ready graduation, standardized test results, state-defined CCR indicators), EL access to college prep curriculum (i.e., Advanced Placement, International Baccalaureate, dual enrollment for college credit), EL postsecondary outcomes, percentage of ELs, total enrollment, student race/ethnicity summaries, and free and reduced lunch percentage.

    b. For each state and/or district, our research team then
       identified a subset of schools that had demonstrated stronger
       than average academic outcomes when compared to similar
       EL population samples at the district or state level.

2. At the same time, we created an online system where individuals
   could nominate schools that have demonstrated success with ELs.
   Within that nomination form, we asked nominators to address the
   following set of questions as applicable to their school site:

    a. Describe the success of the school in terms of traditional
       measures (e.g., academic achievement test scores, EL rate
       of reclassification, graduation rates) and/or nontraditional
       measures (e.g., measures of social-emotional well-being,
       community engagement, special awards).

    b. How is the school organized to support ELs' academic
       language development? How are courses organized for ELs?
       What types of collaborations take place among staff, such as
       between academic content and ESL/ELD specialists? Is there
       shared learning time within the master schedule? How do
       teachers grow their professional expertise?

    c. In what ways does the school support ELs' academic language
       development together with preparing them for college, career,
       and community readiness?

    d. Describe the school culture and climate. How does the school
       leverage the cultural and language assets of the students and
       the community? How is the school staffed to reflect and
       respect the students' cultural and linguistic makeup?

    e. Is there a clear and ambitious mission and vision that shapes
       the school's work with ELs? Describe the school's mission and
       vision. How does the leadership support this mission and/or
       vision?

3. We also reached out within our local Understanding Language
   network of colleagues and asked them to contribute potential
   school sites that our team would consider as a possible case study
   school. These colleagues included researchers, practitioners, and
   policymakers working in the field to advance knowledge about EL
   education, and/or working directly with ELs or EL educators.

4. From the online-nomination process and our outreach among our
   networked colleagues, we received a total of 80 unique school
   nominations from the field. Our team then took the list of 80
   schools and eliminated nominated schools that did not have strong
   quantitative academic and postsecondary outcome measures for
   ELs, had fewer than 10 ELs in their most recent graduating cohort,
   or had less than 5% ELs in their high school program.

Combining the steps 1 through 4 gave us a sample of 28 schools with a range of geographical distribution across the country. From this list of 28 schools, we compiled qualitative school profiles that included specific program design related to ELs, school mission and vision, and student demographics. This information was gathered through online research. Once we created these school profiles, we narrowed the sample by identifying a set of 10 schools that had strong achievement and college-going outcomes for ELs; demonstrated a vision, history, and commitment to educating the diversity of ELs through their school culture and practices; represented a range of program models; represented a range of geographic locations; and had student bodies representing a range of socioeconomic and racial/ethnic backgrounds.

Our team invited each of the 10 schools to submit preliminary information to help us further narrow down our pool of schools. Of the 10 schools, two schools declined participation, and one school was not responsive. In the end we focused our efforts on seven schools across three states, and we had informal phone conversations with these schools' leaders so that we could better understand how they designed and cultivated learning opportunities for the diversity of ELs at their sites.

Our team arranged site visits with each of the seven schools. Of these seven high schools, five schools are located in New York City, one is located in Boston, and one is located in a rural district in California. Though we did complete a site visit at the California school, we ultimately chose not to profile it in the report due to a lack of reliable EL reclassification data to compare to all California schools. The six schools ultimately profiled are Boston International High School and Newcomers Academy (Boston, MA), High School for Dual Language and Asian Studies (Manhattan, NY), It Takes a Village Academy (Brooklyn, NY), Manhattan Bridges (Manhattan, NY), Marble Hill School for International Studies (Bronx, NY), and New World High School (Bronx, NY). A snapshot of the schools' demographics, mission statements, and achievement outcomes is presented in Appendix C.

QUALITATIVE DATA COLLECTION

During the spring of 2014, teams of researchers conducted intensive site visits to each of the seven schools. In preparation for these visits, our team developed protocols for classroom observations, interviews, and focus groups built around gathering evidence on our two key research questions stated earlier. Our team worked closely with the school site liaisons (either the principal or an assistant principal) to coordinate the scheduling of interviews, focus groups, classroom visits, and general logistics of the site visits. Site visitors took notes during the interviews, focus groups, and classroom observations, and our team worked together after the site visits to address any contents of the notes that were unclear or that lacked sufficient detail.

At the end of each visit, the site visit team also wrote up two or three pages of debrief notes that highlighted unique and salient practices of the school pertaining to ELs. Each site visit team also joined the full research team on a one-hour debriefing phone call within one week of the site visit. In addition to the fieldnotes taken during the visit, the summary notes and the notes from the debriefing phone call were considered as part of the qualitative data for each school. The section that follows details the types, depth, and quantity of data sources we collected during our visits.

QUALITATIVE DATA SOURCES:
ANALYSIS OF SCHOOL CULTURE, DESIGN, AND PRACTICES

Our data sources came from three key sources: interviews and focus groups, classroom and school observations, and documents and artifacts provided by the school and available online. Interviews and focus groups were requested with the principal (one interview at the beginning and one at the end of the visit), teachers of ELs, district (and in NYC, network) supervisors, families, alumni, students, as well as any other school staff whose work was highly relevant to ELs or their families (these typically included counselors, assistant principals, and coaches). Some data also were gleaned through informal communication with school leaders preceding and following the site visits.

After the site visits were completed, the research team met as a full team in an all-day meeting to discuss key themes and trends found within each school site and began to identify salient evidence to help us answer our two key research questions. With a broad outline of key themes at hand, the writing team organized and coded the evidence thematically and wrote in-depth cases for each school. The writers shared drafts with the site visiting teams and the full research team, revised the drafts based on feedback, sent the drafts to the schools' leaders (principal and usually assistant principal as well) for review and feedback, and revised them based on schools' feedback. Once the case studies were completed, our team analyzed the cases as a set to determine key takeaways and important lessons to be identified within our larger report.

Educational Policy Contexts of New York City and Boston Public Schools

This appendix is intended to provide information on the policy contexts of the New York City and Boston public schools so readers can understand how the schools in our study operated and developed within their local contexts over time.

NEW YORK CITY EDUCATIONAL CONTEXT

Regional Structures and Small School Reform

Between 2003 and 2010, Mayor Michael Bloomberg and Chancellor Joel Klein embarked on a massive reform effort known as the Children First Initiative. At that time New York City Public Schools were under mayoral control. Facing the reality of a decades-long 50% city graduation rate, they created this initiative to institute better and more equitable academic outcomes. Under Children First, the city's school governance systems and the schools themselves were fundamentally restructured. The school boards were shut down and 10 regions of 120 demographically mixed schools were created. Regional superintendents were hired by the mayor to oversee school improvement efforts. Over this time, the city's education policy resulted in the closure of many large, poor-performing public schools, and increasingly favored small schools, some of which were funded by the Gates Foundation. The city also instituted required core ELA and math curricula tied to increased accountability practices across schools, and invested heavily in their implementation. In addition, teacher pay increased, and recruitment and hiring practices were revamped. An academy to train principals to reinvigorate struggling schools was established, and principals were given more autonomy in teacher hiring and allocation of resources for the most high-needs students. In return, principal performance reviews were implemented and tied to reward systems. Policies were implemented whereby high school students could choose the schools they apply to, and schools effectively competed for students.

Common Core State Standards Implementation and Bilingual Common Core Initiative

Other important changes that have been implemented in New York City in recent years include the adoption of the Common Core State Standards, as well as the launching of the Bilingual Common Core Initiative to develop new English as a Second Language and Native Language Arts Standards aligned to the Common Core. According to the New York State Bilingual Common Core Initiative, standards that have been developed as part of the aforementioned initiative "provide points of entry for students of all language proficiency and literacy levels to access grade level Language Arts content as described by the new New York State Common Core Learning Standards" (Engage New York, 2012, p.1). These standards are now called New Language Arts Progressions (NLAP) and Home Language Arts Progressions (HLP).

Blueprint for English Language Learners Success

The *Blueprint for English Language Learners Success*, produced by the New York State Education Department (NYSED, 2014), is a set of principles intended to guide educators to prepare ELs for college and career readiness beginning in prekindergarten and continuing until high school graduation. This blueprint assumes that *all* teachers are teachers of ELs and must design and deliver appropriate instruction for them. It also assigns responsibility to school and district leaders for meeting ELs' needs. It states that educators and school and district leaders are responsible for delivering instruction that is grade-appropriate, academically rigorous, and aligned with the CCSS.

Bilingualism and biliteracy are judged as assets, and the blueprint requires that schools provide opportunities for second language development and academic language development in the students' home languages. Educators should engage families as partners in their children's education. The expertise of EL educators and professionals should be leveraged to increase the professional capacities of all teachers in this area. According to the blueprint, ELs' language, culture, and prior knowledge should also be leveraged as instructional assets. Finally, instructional practices should be informed by appropriate assessments of students' proficiencies and needs.

Regents Exams

Developed and administered by the New York State Education Department, the Regents exams are the state's elementary and secondary standardized tests required for a Regents diploma. For higher-performing students, they may earn an "Advanced" or an "Honor" designation on their Regents diploma. Some educators have used this set of assessments as a form of college and career readiness indicators.

Institutional Support for ELs

The former Chancellor of New York City's Department of Education (NYC-DOE), Carmen Fariña, created a new position entitled Senior Executive Director of the Department of English Language Learners and Student Support, with the objective of closing the achievement gap between ELs and English proficient students. The NYCDOE Department of English Language Learners and Student Support offers multiple resources, including a high-quality professional development series, Common Core–aligned lesson samples and documents, and a library of resources for their educators. Three years earlier, in 2011, the NYCDOE developed a comprehensive plan to support ELs that promises to increase the number of bilingual teachers and programs, provide timely language proficiency screening, hold principals accountable for EL progress, and increase parental choice options.

In 2012, Governor Andrew Cuomo signed a bill to recognize bilingual and biliterate students by awarding them a Seal of Biliteracy upon graduation. This bill may encourage schools to see the efficacy of using two languages as instructional tools, and to see the value of multilingualism.

BOSTON PUBLIC SCHOOLS CONTEXT

Boston is one of the most diverse public school systems in the country. Nearly half of its students speak a language other than English at home, one-third are considered limited English proficient, and students hail from over 135 different countries. Poverty is high—70% of the student population are categorized as "economically disadvantaged," participating in one or more state-sponsored assistance programs (i.e., Supplemental Nutrition Assistance Program (SNAP), Transitional Aid to Families with Dependent Children (TAFDC), Department of Children and Families (DCF) Foster Care, and MassHealth) (Boston Public Schools, 2016).

Reform of Governance and Structures

Much like the New York City Department of Education, the Boston Public Schools (BPS) came under mayoral control in 1992, and Superintendents Thomas W. Payzant, Michael G. Contompasis, and Carol R. Johnson led the district in steady academic improvements. Tommy Chang is the most recently appointed superintendent.

To drive reform, Boston created a series of pilot schools with school-based autonomy in staffing, curriculum, scheduling, professional learning, and allocation of resources. At the same time, the district increased accountability measures through performance benchmarks. BPS also offers families a choice of a variety of high school options, in what they call a "managed portfolio approach" (Tung & Ouimette, 2007). These school options are intended to provide students with personalized learning environments and high-quality instruction.

Ensuring Equal Opportunities for ELs

In October 2010, Boston Public Schools reached a settlement agreement with the U.S. Department of Justice to ensure equal opportunities for ELs as required by the Equal Educational Opportunities Act of 1974 and Title VI of the Civil Rights Act of 1964. The U.S. Department of Justice issued the following statement on October 1, 2010:

> The Boston Public Schools agreed to assess the English proficiency of an estimated 7,000 students who were not previously tested in all four language domains of listening, speaking, reading and writing, and to ensure that all potential EL students are properly identified and accurately assessed in the 2010–11 school year. In order to serve its EL population, the Boston Public Schools agreed to provide ELL students with Sheltered English Immersion in their core content classes, such as math, social studies and science; to deliver English as a Second Language instruction consistent with state guidance; and to train and hire a sufficient number of teachers to serve its ELL population.

An assistant superintendent was appointed to oversee the Office of English Learners (OEL), and an English Learners' Task Force was formed. This team has since improved assessment and placement practices, prioritized fiscal resources, and strengthened teacher training and programs to address the disparities of educational outcomes for ELs. The OEL vision is as follows:

> to provide a culturally and linguistically responsive education with the supports needed to ensure equitable access to opportunities that promote language acquisition, bilingualism, biliteracy and lifelong learning. (Boston Public Schools, Office of English Learners, 2017)

To meet this vision, BPS has invested more than $10 million to expand EL services and enact extensive reforms. They describe some of their accomplishments and goals:

- We have increased the capacity of programs just for English learners.
- We are working toward establishing Sheltered English Instruction (SEI) programs in schools that are closer to the communities where students live.
- We have changed student assignment rules for ELs. All English language learners are offered SEI programming and guaranteed language development services.
- We are preparing more teachers to effectively teach our English language learners.
- We are identifying and purchasing appropriate materials to better serve English language learners.
- We have opened Newcomers Academy to serve newly arrived, high school age English language learners, and expanded language testing and counseling about school choices at the Newcomers Assessment and Counseling Center.
- We are working to create and maintain a welcoming school climate for English language learners.

As a result of these improvement efforts, both graduation rates and standardized test (MCAS) scores have improved over time for ELs in the Boston Public Schools.

School Profiles

BOSTON INTERNATIONAL HIGH SCHOOL
AND NEWCOMERS ACADEMY

Located in the Dorchester neighborhood of Boston, BINcA was the only high school in the district as of 2013–14 designed to exclusively serve new immigrants and Students with Interrupted Formal Education (SIFE). All of BINcA's students are ELs or recently reclassified former ELs (see Table C.1), and they represent over 40 countries and over 25 language backgrounds (predominantly Spanish, Cape Verdean Creole, and Haitian Creole). Most of their students and families are immigrants living in Dorchester, Roxbury, and Mattapan. Across these working-class communities, many of the students and family members have endured hardship in their home countries and in their journeys to the United States as newly arrived immigrants or as refugees.

Vision

On the public school website, Boston International High School and Newcomers Academy states: "We prepare our students to be empowered, contributing citizens in a global society through a journey of discovery and wonder. Our school community reflects the core values of community, advocacy, diversity, and high expectations. As a community of learners we are becoming a center of excellence in the education of English Language Learners and a resource to others committed to this work" ("About BINCA," n.d.).

Mission

Their public school website also notes the mission of the school: "Boston International Newcomers Academy is a Boston Public School that embraces new immigrant adolescent English language learners and their families. We teach English Language Learners across the content areas while cultivating native language literacy and culture. We partner with our families and community to ensure students will be college and career ready and motivated

Table C.1. Demographics and Performance Data for Boston International High School and Newcomers Academy (2014–15)

2014–15 October Enrollment	4-year Adjusted Cohort Graduation Rate* (2015)
Size: 381	Size: 32
African American: 43%	EL: 100% of the 2011 entry cohort
Hispanic: 50.7%	Graduated: 78.1% (compared to 61.8% Boston graduation rate for ELs)
White: 1.3%	**5-year Adjusted Cohort Graduation Rate (2014)**
Multi-Race, Non-Hispanic: 1.3%	
English not First Language: 100%	Size: 43
English Learner: 83.7%	EL: 100% of the 2010 entry cohort
Students with Disabilities: 3.7%	Graduated: 81.4% (compared to 70.6% Boston graduation rate for ELs)
Note: Individual students may be included in multiple categories.	**Graduates Attending Institutions of Higher Education (2012–13)**
	Size: 58
	EL: 100% of 2012 graduates
	Attending college/university: 77.6%

*The four-year adjusted cohort graduation rate is the number of students who graduate in 4 years with a regular high school diploma divided by the number of students who form the adjusted cohort for the graduating class.
Source: profiles.doe.mass.edu

to pursue a life of learning and civic engagement by instilling the habits of ownership, perseverance, expression, and service" ("About BINCA," n.d.).

Language Development Framework

At Boston International, literacy and language development permeate all classrooms, and every teacher is a teacher of language and content. Students' home languages are assets in their learning, and teacher collaboration is viewed as essential for aligning practices to build students' language and disciplinary skills simultaneously.

Distinctive School Design Features

- Two programs are housed under one school: Boston International High School provides a college preparatory curriculum specifically for ELs, and the Newcomers Academy serves ELs who are recent immigrants.
- Newly arrived ELs in the Newcomers Academy take part in one of two programs before starting high school: High Intensity Language

Training (HILT), targeted toward students who have had interrupted formal education (SIFE) or very limited prior schooling experience, and Sheltered English Immersion (SEI) for all other students. SIFE are enrolled in small classes with significant instruction in their native language.

- Extended learning time after school and on weekends provides students with intensive academic support within an "all-hands-on-deck" learning environment.
- A diverse teaching staff reflects the linguistic and cultural diversity of the student population.

HIGH SCHOOL FOR DUAL LANGUAGE AND ASIAN STUDIES

Situated at the nexus of two neighborhoods, the Lower East Side and Chinatown, in Manhattan, New York City, the High School for Dual Language and Asian Studies (HSDLAS) is deeply committed that all students will comprehend, speak, read, and write in both English and Mandarin Chinese by the time they graduate. Students at the school are predominantly Asian and socioeconomically disadvantaged; almost a quarter of the students are ELs (see Table C.2).

Mission/Vision

On the school website's Fact Sheet, HSDLAS reveals their mission/vision: "High School for Dual Language and Asian Studies is dedicated to preparing its students to meet the challenges of the 21st century. We are devoted to providing quality instruction and guidance counseling to promote the academic and social development of our students as well as their linguistic capacity, cultural appreciation, and international and global awareness. Our goal is for each of our students to grow intellectually, morally, socially, culturally and personally so they are ready for the next stage of their education and to realize their full potential" ("About HSDLAS," n.d.).

Language Development Framework

At HSDLAS, school staff believe that lessons should build on students' cultural backgrounds, lived experiences, and home languages to support students' development in both English and Chinese. Academic discourse serves as a lever for developing students' oral language. Meanwhile, they make use of intentional grouping of students based on their language proficiencies to promote confidence and autonomy, while allowing students access to advance content and language learning.

Table C.2. Demographics and Performance Data for High School for Dual Language and Asian Studies (2014-15)

DEMOGRAPHICS	
Size	416
Asian	89%
African American	3%
Hispanic	6%
White	2%
Multi-Race, Non-Hispanic	1%
English Learner	24%
Free/Reduced Priced Lunch	89%
Students with Disabilities	2%

COLLEGE & CAREER READINESS				
	School	Borough	City	State
4-year Graduation Rate	93%	69%	67%	78%
4-year EL Graduation Rate	96%	35%	37%	34%
College Enrollment Rate	90%	56%	53%	—
College Readiness Rate	81%	39%	35%	—

Note: The demographics and performance data in Tables C.2–C.6 are from two sources: schools.nyc.gov and data.nysed.gov. Each school table shows the following:

- 4-year June graduation rates—Graduates are defined as those students earning either a Local or Regents diploma and exclude those earning either a special education (IEP) diploma or GED.
- College enrollment rate—Percentage of students who graduated from high school and enrolled in a college or postsecondary program within six months.
- College readiness rate—Percentage of students who met the City University of New York's standards for avoiding remedial classes; see schools.nyc.gov.

Distinctive School Design Features

- Dual Language is designed to advance the goal of biliteracy (in English and Chinese) and college readiness for all students.
- A strong administration has assembled teaching staff with strong content knowledge, deep experience working with ELs, and strength in a bilingual setting.
- The course sequence is designed to maximize dual language fluency and college readiness, and is adjusted based on data pertaining to the strengths and needs of the current student body.

- Robust and well-staffed student support services provide students and families with individual attention in the college planning and application process.

IT TAKES A VILLAGE ACADEMY

It Takes A Village Academy is situated in the diverse neighborhood of East Flatbush in Brooklyn, New York. In the past few decades, waves of West Indian immigrants have moved into this neighborhood. This working-class community is predominantly Black and foreign-born, primarily from the Caribbean. ITAVA reflects the demographics of the neighborhood, with a similarly diverse student body (see Table C.3). Students at the school are mostly from Haiti, Jamaica, Trinidad, Guyana, and Spanish-speaking countries, and some also have come from Yemen, Madagascar, Bangladesh, and Uzbekistan. Most students are recent immigrants with U.S. education levels of middle school or below. Approximately a fifth of ITAVA's students are designated as ELs. This population is highly complex, representing different levels of language proficiency, socioeconomic status, academic experience, and immigration history.

Table C.3. Demographics and Performance Data for It Takes A Village Academy (2014–15)

DEMOGRAPHICS			
Size	566		
Asian	1%		
African American	90%		
Hispanic	6%		
White	1%		
English Learner	20%		
Free/Reduced Priced Lunch	80%		
Students with Disabilities	13%		
COLLEGE & CAREER READINESS			
	School	Borough	City	State
4-year Graduation Rate	88%	67%	67%	78%
4-year EL Graduation Rate	89%	36%	37%	34%
College Enrollment Rate	79%	53%	53%	—
College Readiness Rate	19%	34%	35%	—

Mission

As reported in the annual High School Quality Snapshot, the mission of It Takes A Village Academy is to "help students gain academic skills and knowledge, promote an understanding of, and respect for, diverse cultures and languages, support active and responsible citizenship, and inspire in our students a lifelong love of learning and pursuit of excellence. In keeping with our three core values of communication, character and critical thinking, all students study and will become proficient in a foreign language, participate in an advisory group focused on character development and community building and participate in meaningful discussions and projects that will engage their critical thinking and problem-solving skills" ("It Takes A Village Academy High School Quality Snapshot," 2013–14).

Language Development Framework

Teachers at ITAVA can be seen using developmentally and culturally appropriate teaching strategies, coupled with appropriate scaffolding, to allow students to access challenging, discipline-specific content. Intentional grouping and paring strategies also maximize meaningful opportunities for interaction and language practice among students. Supporting the development of students' reading and writing skills is the domain of the content teachers at ITAVA.

Distinctive School Design Features

- The entire school culture revolves around the commitment to providing students with a rich college-preparatory curriculum while leveraging students' cultural and linguistic assets.
- ITAVA customizes each student's schedule according to the student's needs, using deliberate structures such as small classes, block scheduling, extended learning time, and advisories to support all students in mastering college-preparatory coursework.
- Students are offered emotional support and advocacy through a well-developed and effective advisory program, with a student-to-teacher ratio of 10 to 1. Upon enrollment, students are assigned to an advisory teacher for the remainder of their high school careers.
- Significant support for professional learning and collaboration time has translated to low attrition rates within the teaching staff.

MANHATTAN BRIDGES HIGH SCHOOL

Over 2,000 high school students converge from as far away as the Bronx to a large, rectangular, redbrick building in the Hell's Kitchen neighborhood of Manhattan every morning. After checking in at the front desk, approximately a quarter of these students go past the glass-enclosed kitchen of the culinary high school and make their way to Manhattan Bridges High School on the third floor. Like many smaller schools in New York City, Manhattan Bridges shares a building with five other high schools. The students are all Latino/Hispanic and qualify for free or reduced priced lunch, and are predominately ELs or former ELs (see Table C.4).

Mission/Vision

Manhattan Bridges boasts the following mission/vision: "We are a New Visions School founded on the belief that mastery of communication skills in both English and students' native language is key to realizing a student's potential in a multicultural society. We are committed to assisting students in maintaining the richness of their native language and culture and celebrating their individual differences, while providing them with a sense of place in their community and society as a whole. Our mission is to ensure that students develop the bilingual speaking, reading, writing and listening skills designed to prepare them for higher education and/or the work force" ("Manhattan Bridges High School Quality Snapshot," 2013–14).

Table C.4. Demographics and Performance Data for Manhattan Bridges High School (2014–15)

DEMOGRAPHICS			
Size	529		
Asian	0%		
African American	0%		
Hispanic	100%		
White	0%		
English Learner	53%		
Students with Interrupted Formal Education	41%		
Free/Reduced Priced Lunch	100%		
Students with Disabilities	2%		
COLLEGE & CAREER READINESS			
	School	Borough	City	State
4-year Graduation Rate	92%	69%	67%	78%
4-year EL Graduation Rate	85%	35%	37%	34%
College Enrollment Rate	68%	56%	53%	—
College Readiness Rate	42%	39%	35%	—

Language Development Framework

At Manhattan Bridges, students are expected to graduate as fully bilingual and biliterate users of academic registers in both English and Spanish. The practice of translanguaging allows students to maneuver fluidly between languages and draw from either language to solidify their understanding of academic content. Classrooms should be language-rich environments in which language and content are integrated, and scaffolds are put in place to support students' use of language to access rigorous content.

Distinctive School Design Features

- Manhattan Bridges High School was designed from the outset to be a school that prepares ELs to be college- and career-ready, as well as fully bilingual and biliterate in academic Spanish and English.
- The school offers two STEM academies, in engineering and IT. Students can apply to either the Transitional Bilingual Program (for newly arrived native Spanish speakers) or the Dual Language Spanish Program.
- The school uses each student's educational history and assessment results to design an individualized educational program, and frequently adjusts the student's placement based on his or her progress.
- A careful teacher candidate screening process—coupled with a thoughtful process of orienting new teachers to the school's values, cultures, and expectations—creates a dedicated, experienced, and flexible teaching community that embraces a mindset of continuous improvement.

MARBLE HILL HIGH SCHOOL

Marble Hill High School is located in the Bronx. It is a small but highly diverse school (see Table C.5). Its student body speaks over 35 different languages and represents 49 countries from around the world. The languages spoken most commonly by students at the school include Spanish, French, Arabic, Bengali, and several African languages.

Mission

As expressed on their public school website, the mission of Marble Hill is as follows: "To develop in each student the necessary skills to acquire and apply knowledge. Students will be provided with a social, emotional, and physical environment that is nurturing, supportive, intellectually challenging, and conducive to learning. Students will be empowered to become

Table C.5. Demographics and Performance Data for Marble Hill High School (2014–15)

DEMOGRAPHICS	
Size	449
Asian	9%
African American	24%
Hispanic	61%
White	5%
English Learner	30%
Free/Reduced Priced Lunch	91%
Students with Disabilities	9%

COLLEGE & CAREER READINESS				
	School	Borough	City	State
4-year Graduation Rate	92%	58%	67%	78%
4-year EL Graduation Rate	75%	38%	37%	34%
College Enrollment Rate	77%	43%	53%	—
College Readiness Rate	62%	22%	35%	—

self-directed, life-long learners inspired by their personal quest for understanding of themselves and the global society in which they live" ("About Marble Hill School for International Studies," n.d.).

Language Development Framework

At Marble Hill, diversity of languages and cultures is an asset to be celebrated, and all students graduate having learned a second or third language. It is the belief of the school that language and literacy practices should be folded into content teaching and learning across classrooms. They utilize project-based learning projects to assess students' language and content learning in meaningful and rigorous ways.

Distinctive School Design Features

- Marble Hill provides an educational experience focused on international studies, actively creating an environment that allows students from varied cultural, national, and linguistic backgrounds to thrive.
- The school has a proactive intake process to recruit a diverse student body of 30% ELs and 50% English proficient students. Marble Hill also offers two different types of programs, the ESL and International

strands, to target support and services to its diverse student body (see Table C.5).

- Instruction is strongly focused on a project-based, inquiry approach to learning; portfolio presentations occur twice a year, every year, in every course, for every grade level.
- Most teachers at Marble Hill are ESL-certified, have travel experience outside the country, and speak another language, and many served in the Peace Corps or the Japan Exchange and Teaching (JET) Program.

NEW WORLD HIGH SCHOOL

Located in the Bronx, New World High School is home to a flourishing community of individuals. With a student body that represents 40 countries and 20 languages, it is a beacon of diversity that boasts extraordinary results for its population of ELs (see Table C.6). Students at the school come from all over the world—including Ecuador, the Dominican Republic, Nigeria, El Salvador, and many other countries—and some students speak

Table C.6. Demographics and Performance Data for New World High School (2014-15)

DEMOGRAPHICS	
Size	408
Asian	14%
African American	9%
Hispanic	66%
White	8%
English Learner	63%
Newcomer	23%
Former EL	27%
Students with Interrupted Formal Education (SIFE)	19%
Free/Reduced Priced Lunch	95%
Students with Disabilities	6%

COLLEGE & CAREER READINESS				
	School	Borough	City	State
4-year Graduation Rate	88%	58%	67%	78%
4-year EL Graduation Rate	77%	38%	37%	34%
College Enrollment Rate	59%	43%	53%	—
College Readiness Rate	45%	22%	35%	—

three or four languages. Additionally, there is variety in terms of prior levels of schooling. Back in their home countries, students may have attended a private or public school, or none at all. Furthermore, students arrive with different proficiency levels in their home languages.

Mission

As stated on their website, New World's mission is the following: "To help our students adapt to their new surroundings and to explore their new country. To help them improve the skills they bring with them and to help them develop new skills to be able to succeed as global citizens. And, with the focused support of our team, our students will be able to exceed New York State Graduation Standards" ("New World High School Mission," n.d.).

Language Development Framework

New World believes lessons in all disciplines should integrate language and content. Content and language objectives, used consistently across classrooms, facilitate learning for ELs and allow students to assess their own levels of understanding and improvement. The school's approach of using the home language in earlier grades allows students to transition to more English as they progress in their English proficiency.

Distinctive School Design Features

- New World is a school designed specifically for ELs: as stated on the school website, it is "centered around the language acquisition needs of all students in all subjects" to ensure that all students acquire and develop "the skills necessary for success by infusing ESL into all content areas of instruction" (schools.nyc.gov/SchoolPortals/11/X513/AboutUs/Overview/default.htm).
- The practice of looping allows most students to be taught generally by the same content teachers all four years, allowing for consistency and accountability.
- Constant reevaluation of instruction, frequent teacher collaboration and intervisitations, feedback from peers and administrators, and numerous professional development opportunities allow the school to continuously improve teaching practice. Administrators encourage teachers to conduct action research to reflect on their practice and build their instructional leadership.
- New World maintains thoughtful and strategic partnerships with external organizations, such as Fordham University's Center for Educational Partnerships, to pursue goals aligned to the school mission.

Key Concepts Defined

College and Career Readiness (CCR)—While a variety of definitions for college and career readiness exist, we use the term broadly to mean that a high school graduate has the academic and social-emotional skills and knowledge that profiled schools believe are necessary to enter college without remediation and to succeed in college and careers.

English Learner (EL)—An individual who is in the process of actively learning English and whose primary language is one other than English.

English Proficient (EP)—Students who have never been classified as ELs or who were formerly ELs but have been reclassified.

Language Development Framework—People's best thinking (which is informed by research and practice) about how students' languages develop; the theory of language learning that permeates the school.

Leadership—The educators who create, refine, and sustain practices and structures in the school community to ensure shared responsibility and accountability for student success.

Learning Design—The way that educators in the school organize and enact the entire instructional experience; practices that are enacted intentionally in all classrooms (e.g., use of students' cultural and linguistic resources, scaffolding, instructional tasks, assessment, pacing, grouping); the teaching and learning coherence within the school.

Professional Learning—Learning that educators experience to further and complement their existing professional skills. May occur in conventional professional development settings; in community with peers, mentors, study groups or networks; as part of action research; on the job; or outside the work setting.

Programming—The strategic ways in which schools create specialized schedules and course sequences for CCR (e.g., newcomer academy, length of the period/course to match the needs of the students) and place students into those for language, academic, or social-emotional purposes.

Reclassified—Refers to former ELs who have met local criteria and are now considered to be English Proficient.

Structures—The way in which schools allocate and organize time, resources, and staff to ensure that students have CCR (e.g., ESL is done in an integrated ESL/ELA block; looping, in which the same teacher follows his or her students through several grades; common staff planning time).

Education Acronyms

AP—Advanced Placement
CBI—College Bound Initiative
CCR—College and Career Readiness
CCSS—Common Core State Standards
CRC—College Readiness Class
CUNY—City University of New York
DLL—Dual Language Learner
ELA—English Language Arts
ELD—English Language Development
EL—English Learner
ELL—English Language Learner
EP—English Proficient
ESL—English as a Second Language
ESSA—Every Student Succeeds Act
HILT—High Intensity Literacy Training
MCAS—Massachusetts Comprehensive Assessment System
MLL—Multilingual Learner
LTEL—Long-term English Learner
NGSS—Next Generation Science Standards
NYSESLAT—New York State English as Second Language Achievement
    Test
OER—Open Educational Resources
QTEL—Quality Teaching for English Learners
RAELs—Recently Arrived English Learners
SEI—Sheltered English Instruction
SIFE—Students with Interrupted Formal Education
SIOP—Sheltered Instruction Observation Protocol

References

About BINCA. (n.d.). Retrieved from bostonpublicschools.org/domain/1823

About HSDLAS. (n.d.). Retrieved from hsdlas.org/about

About Marble Hill School for International Studies. (n.d.) Retrieved from marble-hillschool.org/about/aboutus.html

Acaroglu, L. (2013, May 4). Where do old cellphones go to die? *The New York Times*. Retrieved from nytimes.com/2013/05/05/opinion/sunday/where-do-old-cellphones-go-to-die.html

Achebe, C. (1994). *Things fall apart*. New York, NY: Anchor Books.

Alvarez, L., Ananada, S., Walqui, A., Sato, E., & Rabinowitz, S. (2014). *Focusing formative assessments on the needs of English Language Learners*. San Francisco, CA: WestEd.

Barron, B., & Darling-Hammond, L. (2008). *Teaching for meaningful learning: A review of research on inquiry-based and cooperative learning*. San Rafael, CA: George Lucas Educational Foundation. Retrieved from edutopia.org/pdfs/edutopia-teaching-for-meaningful-learning.pdf

Barron, B. J. S., Schwartz, D. L., Vye, N. J., Moore, A., Petrosino, A., Zech, L., Bransford, J. D., & The Cognition and Technology Group at Vanderbilt. (1998). Doing with understanding: Lessons from research on problem- and project-based learning. *The Journal of the Learning Sciences, 7*(3–4), 271–311.

Bass, B. M., & Riggio, R. E. (2006). *Transformational leadership*. Mahwah, NJ: Lawrence Erlbaum Associates.

Black, P., & Wiliam, D. (1998). Assessment and classroom learning. *Assessment in Education: Principles, Policy & Practice, 5*(1), 7–74.

Boston Public Schools. (2016, December). Boston Public Schools at a glance. Retrieved from bostonpublicschools.org/Page/689

Boston Public Schools, Office of English Learners. (2017). Retrieved from bostonpublicschools.org/ELL

Bryk, A. S. (2010). Organizing schools for improvement. *Phi Delta Kappan, 91*(7), 23–30.

Bryk, A. S., Gomez, L. M., Grunow, A., & LeMahieu, P. G. (2015). *Learning to improve: How America's schools can get better at getting better*. Cambridge, MA: Harvard Education Press.

Bryk, A. S., & Schneider, B. (2002). *Trust in schools: A core resource for improvement*. New York, NY: Russell Sage Foundation.

Bryk, A. S., Sebring, P. B., Allensworth, E., Easton, J. Q., & Luppescu, S. (2010). *Organizing schools for improvement: Lessons from Chicago*. Chicago, IL: University of Chicago Press.

Bunch, G., Kibler, A., & Pimentel, S. (2012). Realizing opportunities for English Learners in the Common Core English Language Arts and Disciplinary Literacy Standards. Stanford, CA: Understanding Language, Stanford University. Retrieved from ell.stanford.edu/publication/realizing-opportunities-ells-common-core-english-language-arts-and-disciplinary-literacy

Canady, R. L., & Rettig, M. D. (1995). *Block scheduling: A catalyst for change in high schools.* Princeton, NJ: Eye on Education.

Carnegie Foundation. (2017). How a networked improvement community improved success rates for struggling college math students. Palo Alto, CA: Carnegie Foundation for the Advancement of Teaching. Retrieved from carnegiefoundation.org/resources/publications/how-a-networked-improvement-community-improved-success-rates-for-struggling-college-math-students/

Cervantes, S. M., & Grossman, E. (2003). *Don Quixote de la Mancha.* New York, NY: Ecco.

Council of Chief State School Officers. (2012). Framework for English Language Proficiency Development Standards corresponding to the Common Core State Standards and the Next Generation Science Standards. Washington, DC: Author. Retrieved from ccsso.org/Documents/2012/ELPD%20Framework%20Booklet-Final%20for%20web.pdf

Cuban, L. (1984). Transforming the frog into a prince: Effective schools research, policy, and practice at the district level. *Harvard Educational Review, 54*(2), 129–152.

Danielson, C. (2011). *Enhancing professional practice: A framework for teaching.* Alexandria, VA: Association of Supervision and Curriculum Development.

Darling-Hammond, L. (1997). *The right to learn: A blueprint for creating schools that work.* San Francisco, CA: Jossey-Bass.

Darling-Hammond, L., & Bransford, J. (2007). *Preparing teachers for a changing world: What teachers should learn and be able to do.* San Francisco, CA: Wiley.

Datnow, A., Lasky, S., Stringfield, S., & Teddlie, C. (2006). *Integrating educational systems for successful reform in diverse contexts.* New York, NY: Cambridge University Press.

David, J. L., & Talbert, J. L. (2013). Learning from Sanger: Turning around a high-poverty district. San Francisco, CA: S.H. Cowell Foundation. Retrieved from shcowell.org/wp-content/uploads/2015/12/Learning-From-Sanger.pdf

Durlak, J. A., Weissberg, R. P., Dymnicki, A. B., Taylor, R. D., & Schellinger, K. B. (2011). The impact of enhancing students' social and emotional learning: A meta-analysis of school-based universal interventions. *Child Development, 82*(1), 405–432.

Dweck, C. (2006). *Mindset: The new psychology of success.* New York, NY: Random House.

Elmore, R. F. (2000). *Building a new structure for school leadership.* Washington, DC: Albert Shanker Institute.

Engage New York. (2012). Theoretical foundations of the New York State Bilingual Common Core. Retrieved from engageny.org/resource/new-york-state-bilingual-common-core-initiative/file/135506

Epstein, J. L. (2001). Building bridges of home, school, and community: The importance of design. *Journal of Education for Students Placed at Risk, 6*(1–2), 161–168.

Fang, Z. (2006). The language demands of science reading in middle school. *International Journal of Science Education, 28*(5), 491–520.

Farrington, C. A., Roderick, M., Allensworth, E., Nagaoka, J., Keyes, T. S., Johnson, D. W., & Beechum, N. O. (2012). *Teaching adolescents to become learners: The role of noncognitive factors in shaping school performance—a critical literature review.* Chicago, IL: Consortium on Chicago School Research.

García, O., & Sylvan, C. E. (2011). Pedagogies and practices in multilingual classrooms: Singularities in pluralities. *The Modern Language Journal, 95*(3), 385–400.

Grant, J. (1996). *The looping handbook: Teachers and students progressing together.* Peterborough, NJ: Crystal Springs Books.

Hakuta, K., Butler, Y. G., & Witt, D. (2000). How long does it take English Learners to attain proficiency? The University of California Linguistic Minority Research Institute, Policy Report 2000-1. Retrieved from eric.ed.gov/?id=ED443275

Hallinger, P. (2003). Leading educational change: Reflections on the practice of instructional and transformational leadership. *Cambridge Journal of Education, 33*(3), 329–352.

Hallinger, P. (2005). Instructional leadership and the school principal: A passing fancy that refuses to fade away. *Leadership and Policy in Schools, 4*(3), 221–239.

Hamedani, M. G., & Darling-Hammond, L. (2014). *Social emotional learning in high school: How three urban high schools engage, educate, and empower youth.* Palo Alto, CA: Stanford Center for Opportunity Policy in Education (SCOPE).

Hansberry, L. (1984). *A raisin in the sun.* New York, NY: Samuel French.

Henderson, A. T., & Mapp, K. L. (2002). *A new wave of evidence: The impact of school, family, and community connections on student achievement.* Austin, TX: Southwest Educational Development Laboratory.

Heritage, M. (2007). Formative assessment: What do teachers need to know and do? *Phi Delta Kappan, 89*(2), 140–145.

It Takes A Village Academy High School Quality Snapshot. (2013–14). Retrieved from schools.nyc.gov/OA/SchoolReports/2013-14/School_Quality_Snapshot_2014_HS_K563.pdf

Jeynes, W. H. (2007). The relationship between parental involvement and urban secondary school student academic achievement: A meta-analysis. *Urban Education, 42*(1), 82–110.

Kibler, A., Valdés, G., & Walqui, A. (2014). What does standards-based educational reform mean for English language learner populations in primary and secondary schools? *TESOL Quarterly, 48*(3), 433–453.

Lau v. Nichols, 414 U.S. 563 (1974).

Manhattan Bridges High School Quality Snapshot. (2013–14). Retrieved from schools.nyc.gov/OA/SchoolReports/2013-14/School_Quality_Snapshot_2014_HS_M542.pdf

McKeown, M. G., Beck, I. L., Omanson, R. C., & Pople, M. T. (1985). Some effects of the nature and frequency of vocabulary instruction on the knowledge and use of words. *Reading Research Quarterly, 20*(5), 522–535.

National Center on Universal Design for Learning. (2015). About Universal Design for Learning. Retrieved from udlcenter.org/aboutudl

National Research Council. (2001). *Knowing what students know: The science and design of educational assessment.* Washington, DC: National Academies Press.

National Research Council. (2012). *Education for life and work: Developing transferable knowledge and skills in the 21st century.* Washington, DC: The National Academies Press.

New World High School Mission. (n.d.). Retrieved from newworldhighschool.com/our-mission

New York City Department of Education. (2017). School quality snapshots. Retrieved from schools.nyc.gov/SchoolPortals/18/K563/AboutUs/Statistics/default.htm

New York State Education Department, Office of Bilingual Education and World Languages. (2014). Blueprint for English language learners success. Retrieved from nysed.gov/common/nysed/files/programs/bilingual-ed/nysblueprintforell-success.2016.pdf

Noddings, N. (2012). *Peace education: How we come to love and hate war.* New York, NY: Cambridge University Press.

Noddings, N. (2015). *The challenge to care in schools* (2nd ed.). New York, NY: Teachers College Press.

Ovando, C. J., Collier, V. P., & Combs, M. C. (2003). *Bilingual and ESL classrooms: Teaching in multicultural contexts.* Boston, MA: McGraw-Hill.

Polman, J., & Pea, R. D. (2006). Transformative communication in project science learning discourse. In R. Horowitz (Ed.), *Talking texts: Knowing the world through the evolution of instructional discourse* (pp. 297–315). New York, NY: Teachers College Press.

Schoenfeld, A. H. (2014). What makes for powerful classrooms, and how can we support teachers in creating them? A story of research and practice, productively intertwined. *Educational Researcher, 43*(8), 404–412.

Spillane, J. P., Halverson, R., & Diamond, J. B. (2001). Investigating school leadership practice: A distributed perspective. *Educational Researcher, 30*(3), 23–28.

Stiggins, R. (2005). From formative assessment to assessment for learning: A path to success in standards-based schools. *Phi Delta Kappan, 87*(4), 324–328.

Thayer, Y. V., & Shortt, T. L. (1999). Block scheduling can enhance school climate. *Educational Leadership, 56*(4), 76–81.

Thomas, J. W. (2000). A review of research on project-based learning. San Rafael, CA: Autodesk Foundation. Retrieved from bie.org/images/uploads/general/9d06758fd346969cb63653d00dca55c0.pdf

Tung, R., & Ouimette, M. (2007). *Strong results, high demand: A four-year study of Boston's pilot high schools.* Boston, MA: The Center for Collaborative Research.

Understanding Language. (2013). Principles for ELL instruction. Retrieved from ell.stanford.edu/content/principles-ell-instruction-january-2013

U.S. Department of Education, National Center for Education Statistics. (2016). State nonfiscal survey of public elementary and secondary education, 2008–09 through 2014–15 [EDFacts file 141, Data Group 678, from the EDFacts Data Warehouse (internal U.S. Department of Education source); Common Core of Data (CCD)]. Retrieved from nces.ed.gov/programs/digest/d16/tables/dt16_204.27.asp

U.S. Department of Education, National Center for Education Statistics. (2017). The condition of education: English language learners in public schools. Retrieved from nces.ed.gov/programs/coe/indicator_cgf.asp

U.S. Department of Education, Office of English Language Acquisition. (2017). Fast Facts. Retrieved from ed.gov/about/offices/list/oela/fast-facts/index.html

U.S. Department of Justice, Office of Public Affairs. (2010, October 1). Departments of Justice and Education reach settlement with Boston School Committee to ensure equal opportunities for ELL students. Washington, DC: U.S. Government Printing Office (Press Release Number: 10-1109).

Valdés, G. (1996). *Con respeto: Bridging the distances between culturally diverse families and schools*. New York, NY: Teachers College Press.

Valdés, G., Kibler, A., & Walqui, A. (2014, March). Changes in the expertise of ESL professionals: Knowledge and action in an era of new standards. Alexandria, VA: TESOL International Association. Retrieved from tesol.org/docs/default-source/papers-and-briefs/professional-paper-26-march-2014.pdf

Walqui, A., & van Lier, L. (2010). *Scaffolding the academic success of adolescent English language learners: A pedagogy of promise*. San Francisco, CA: WestEd.

Wong Fillmore, L., & Snow, C. (2000). *What teachers need to know about language*. Washington, DC: U.S. Department of Education, Office of Educational Research and Improvement.

Index

About the Authors

Martha Castellón Palacios was the executive director for Understanding Language. Martha is an educator, researcher, and advocate for English learners. She served as Palo Alto's equity coordinator and has worked as a classroom teacher. Martha holds both a B.A. and a Ph.D. in Educational Linguistics from Stanford University.

Tina Cheuk researches the development of teaching practices and school structures that support English learners in science classrooms. Tina is a doctoral candidate in Science Education at Stanford University. She holds a B.S. in Chemistry and Biochemistry from the University of Chicago and an M.A. in Policy, Organizations, and Leadership from Stanford University.

Rebecca Greene is a linguistics and education researcher. She received her Ph.D. in Linguistics from Stanford University. Her interests lie in issues of language and equity, with regard to English learners as well as speakers of nonstandard dialects, and with regard to education as well as society more broadly.

Kenji Hakuta is emeritus professor at the Graduate School of Education at Stanford University and is the co-chair of Understanding Language.

Diana Mercado-Garcia researches large-scale policies and how they influence organizational change at the school, state, and federal level to reduce social, economic, and racial inequalities. Diana is a doctoral candidate in Education Policy and Sociology of Education at Stanford University as well as an Institute of Education Sciences (IES) fellow. She holds a B.A. in Sociology and Spanish Linguistics from University of California, Berkeley.

María Santos is the co-chair and senior advisor for leadership at Understanding Language. From 2010–14, Santos served as deputy superintendent for instruction, leadership, and equity-in-action for the Oakland (CA) Unified School District. Prior to 2010, she was the senior instructional manager and superintendent for the Office of English Language Learners at the New York City Department of Education. María is currently the director for school and district services at WestEd.

Renae Skarin is an education researcher and directs the English Learner Success Forum. She was formerly a researcher and project manager for Understanding Language.

Lisa Zerkel was a researcher at Understanding Language. She holds a B.A. in Social Studies from Harvard University and an M.A. in Education from Stanford University.